THE BROKEN HOOP

The aim of Zenith Books is to present the history of minority groups in the United States and their participation in the growth and development of the country. Through histories and biographies written by leading historians in collaboration with established writers for young people, Zenith Books will increase awareness of and at the same time develop an understanding and appreciation for minority group heritage.

DR. JOHN HOPE FRANKLIN, Chairman of the History Department at the University of Chicago, has also taught at Brooklyn College, Fisk University, and Howard University. For the year 1962–63, he was William Pitt Professor of American History and Institutions at Cambridge University in England. He is the author of many books, including *From Slavery to Freedom, The Militant South, Reconstruction After the Civil War*, and *The Emancipation Proclamation*.

DAN GEORGAKAS was born in Detroit, Michigan. He attended Wayne State University, where he received a B.A. degree in history, and the University of Michigan, where he received his M.A. degree. In 1963, Mr. Georgakas was a member of a Fulbright Study group in Greece. His poetry has appeared in the following anthologies: *Where Is Vietnam?, 31 New American Poets, The Now Generation, Campfires of the Resistance, Thunderbolts of Peace and Freedom*, and many more. Currently, Mr. Georgakas is working on a book on the recent history of the city of Detroit and also a novel.

The Broken Hoop

THE HISTORY OF NATIVE AMERICANS FROM 1600 TO 1890, FROM THE ATLANTIC COAST TO THE PLAINS

⫘

Dan Georgakas

ZENITH BOOKS

DOUBLEDAY & COMPANY, INC., GARDEN CITY, NEW YORK

1973

Library of Congress Catalog Card Number 70–175374
Copyright © 1973 by Doubleday & Company, Inc.
All Rights Reserved
Printed in the United States of America
First Edition

The Zenith Books edition, published simultaneously in hardbound and paper-back volumes, is the first publication of *The Broken Hoop*.

Zenith Books Edition: 1973

COVER CREDIT: "The Battle of the Little Bighorn" was painted about 1898 by Kicking Bear, a veteran of the fight. (*Courtesy of the Southwest Museum, Los Angeles, California.*)

CONTENTS

INTRODUCTION

They have left their names upon half the United States and upon a hundred cities and a thousand landmarks, but we do not know them. Columbus called them Indians because he mistakenly thought he had landed on the shores of India. Indians they are still called, but, in fact, they are the Native Americans.

Most scholars believe the Native Americans' ancestors crossed from Siberia to Alaska thousands of years ago by means of what was then either a land bridge or short waterway between Asia and North America. One skull found in California indicates that these people may have been living in North America as early as 20,000 B.C. At another place what appears to be a man-made fireplace dates back to 30,000 B.C.

By the time of Columbus, the Native Americans had developed over two thousand languages and major dialects, more than in all of Europe and Asia. Rather than alphabets, Indians used picture symbols to aid their remarkable memories retain their rich oral tradition of songs, stories, poetry, and rituals. Their eloquence has become renowned. Wherever possible in the pages that follow, the words and expressions of the Native Americans will be used to express their vision. The Mississippi River will be called Father of Waters. Citizens of the United States will be the people of the eagle. Canada during the reign of Queen Victoria will be Queen Grandmother's Land. Concepts such as *forever* will be given in the Indian form *as long as the grass shall grow and the water flow.*

The Native Americans believed the things of the spirit were more important than material things. They believed the earth was their mother and all living things were her children. They believed the universe was bound in a circle of harmony. Their communal spirit emphasized giving rather than receiving. They distrusted any individual seeking personal power. When the European invaders came upon them in a fury of wheels and hoofs, the Indians were stunned. The two cultures were incompatible. The Europeans seemed to have spirits harder than the hardest rocks. The Native Americans were willing to share their continent, but the newcomers wanted it entirely for themselves. The Indians believed the whites were long lost brothers, but the whites considered the Indians to be racially inferior.

War followed war as the whites moved westward across the continent. The Native Americans were forced on reservations far from their ancestral lands. Their traditional ways were torn from them. The animals were killed off. The fish did not return to the rivers. Trees that had stood as long as the oldest man could remember fell. The great unity of the circle was undone; the cycle of life broken. An Iroquois said, "The Tree of Life is uprooted." A Sioux holy man wrote, "The Nation's Hoop is broken." And so it was.

Banks of the Musconetcong
Delaware Country
1973

THE BROKEN HOOP

Black Hawk, leader of the Wisconsin Sauk, had little respect for his white opponents. When he surrendered he said, "The white men do not scalp the head; but they do worse—they poison the heart." (*Huntington Free Library, Heye Foundation*)

PART I

In Search of Unity: The Northeast

I admit that there are good white men, but they bear no proportion to the bad; the bad must be the strongest, for they rule. They do what they please. They enslave those who are not of their color, although created by the same Great Spirit who created them. They would make slaves of us if they could; but as they cannot do it, they kill us. There is no faith to be placed in their words. They are not like the Indians, who are only enemies while at war, and are friends in peace . . . Remember that this day I have warned you to beware of such friends as these. I know the Long Knives. They are not be be trusted. (1787)

Pachgrantschilias (Delaware)

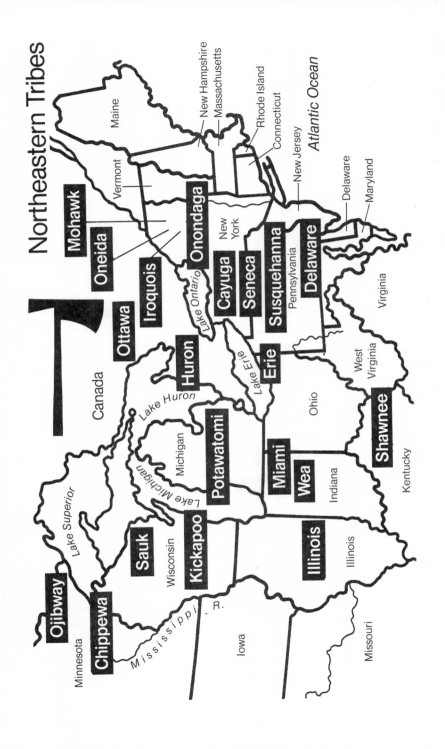

IROQUOIS,
THE RATTLESNAKE PEOPLE

When the Iroquois sang before their fires, they believed they were helping to renew the world by giving strength to Teharonhiawagon, the Master of Life. The Iroquois believed the forest and everything in it was a living thing. Trees and wind and the smallest animals were important. Some creatures were so clever that they were considered to be related to the Creative Force which had made the universe. Songs in late winter, when life was harshest and men sometimes grew desperate in the bitter struggle to survive, were more than entertainment. Songs were a spiritual force that would help bring springtime when the forest would be reborn. Whenever a hunter made a kill, he was careful to leave behind some intestines, bones, or meat to help other creatures survive. Greediness by any individual might cause the spirits to withdraw their favor. Nothing was without meaning. A storm might indicate the spirits were troubled while sunshine was a sure sign they were in a good mood.

At times the forest could be a dangerous place for humans, but it was primarily a place to be loved rather than feared. It was the source of life and every Iroquois was comfortable in it. The forest provided the Iroquois with deer, moose, beaver, bear, and every sort of fowl to hunt. Wild turkeys sometimes ran to forty pounds and pigeons numbered in the millions. Cod, sturgeon, mackerel, and salmon were available in inland waters or in the nearby ocean. Children and women could gather lobsters, crabs, clams, and other shellfish along the beaches or they could enter the forest to get maple sugar, birds' eggs, and berries. As a guarantee that they would never be hungry, the Iroquois used clearings among the trees to plant corn, beans, and squash which they called the Three Sisters.

The Iroquois believed every living thing was filled with a strength called *orenda* and that dreams were the main contact between *orenda* and human understanding. Individuals fasted and prayed in hope of obtaining visions although an unsought vision was the most valuable. The shamans, who were a combination of doctor and priest, were expected to dream often and to know more than most mortals about the wishes of spirits. In midwinter a dream festival was held to strengthen Teharonhiawagon. Old fires were put out and new ones lighted. False face societies made up of men in masks and costumes danced to control the evil spirits which lingered among the trees and caused illness. Men and women sang their best songs so that the snows would melt quickly and the forest blossom as soon as possible.

During times of peace, the Iroquois tended to be mild-mannered and polite individuals who were very kind to their children. Their log homes were from fifty to one hundred feet long and housed up to ten families. Some of the ferocity of their warfare may have stemmed from the frustration of living in houses with only small slits in the ceiling to bring relief from the smoke, dogs, cooking odors, and noises of so many people. Taboos such as not being able to speak with one's mother-in-law made life somewhat easier, but if a couple quarreled the whole family would sit in judgment.

By the time the Europeans arrived in the early 1600s,

the Iroquois had created one of the most democratic systems of government ever invented. The details of this system were so impressive that years later Benjamin Franklin would use them in proposing his Albany Plan for unifying the colonies. Still later, the United States Constitution would incorporate many Iroquois ideas. The League of the Iroquois was made up of the five major Iroquois-speaking people: the Seneca, the Mohawk, the Cayuga, the Oneida, and the Onondaga. Each of these nations had an equal vote in the government although each had several representatives whose number depended on the tribe's population and importance. The representatives were called sachems and they were selected for their wisdom, logic, and eloquence. They wore impressive antelope antlers as symbols of their authority but they never used violence to enforce their decisions. During meetings of the Great Council, four nations voted on all issues while the sachems of the Onondaga acted as chairmen. When decisions were difficult, as was often the case, the Onondaga sachems had the responsibility of presenting the arguments of all sides and proposing workable solutions. Men and women sat for hours listening to their representatives debate complicated ideas until they reached the required unanimous agreement. Oratory had always been an Iroquois art and with the creation of the League, great speakers became as important as great warriors. The Seneca orator Red Jacket who lived during the era of the American Revolution became indignant when asked what he had done as a warrior, "A warrior not! I am an orator! I was born an orator!"

Political power flowed upward from the people rather than downward from the sachems. Some sachems qualified partly through heredity but they had to be voted on by all adult males and females. Other sachems were specifically chosen without regard to heredity to insure representation for all. Warriors were forbidden to be sachems because it was feared they might lead the League into unnecessary wars. Women could not be sachems, but they had the deciding voice in the final selection of sachems which resulted from their central role in the Iroquois social structure.

The family was the basic unit of Iroquois society, providing for personal needs and making most of the decisions directly affecting an individual's life. Fifty to one hundred people usually made up a family and they were under the leadership of the oldest or most respected woman, who automatically headed the family council. All family relationships were traced through the mothers rather than the fathers and women owned the dwellings and planting grounds. Marriages and all other important social activities were under the direct or indirect control of the women. Beyond this family structure was the village council representing a number of families in a small geographical area and beyond the village was the important clan council which overlapped villages to represent related families. The clan councils selected the sachems who represented the nation which was made up of all the villages within an area united by common dialect, custom, marriage, and military interest. Women played a key role at every level and the Iroquois boasted that their prosperity was due to the wisdom and authority of the mothers of the nations.

All national, clan, and village decisions were made in councils. Any of these councils could refuse to be party to any decisions without fear of coercion. Any individual might observe or participate at almost any level although the most persuasive and respected were naturally chosen to be official spokesmen at each higher level of government. The lack of police assured a totally free system although unanimous agreement was desired on important matters and the most strenuous efforts were made to obtain this through debate. Decision making on a League scale could be a slow process but the end result of so many councils was a people united in a way unique among the Indians.

The League was an extraordinary achievement and it showed the most positive aspect of the gifted Iroquois. Life had not always been so orderly or pleasant for the five nations. In the late 1500s, the Iroquois had fallen into what seemed a perpetual winter of the spirit. Fights with rival language groups were constant, and their enemies had been able to push the divided Iroquois from some of the better hunting and planting grounds. Life was a never-ending war—and Iroquois war was a terrible affair of tomahawks shattering the brains of warriors, women, babies, and the old impartially. Captives began to be tortured as they were taken along the trails back to the villages of the victorious raiders. Even greater suffering and almost certain death was in store for all male prisoners. The Europeans had a difficult time understanding how the Iroquois could behave so cruelly during war because they never understood Iroquois religious beliefs.

Wampum belt used to record the end of warfare among the Iroquois and the establishment of the Great Peace. (*Courtesy of Museum of the American Indian, Heye Foundation*)

The Iroquois valued bravery as one of their highest virtues. Even when they tortured a warrior, the Iroquois thought they were giving him a chance for an ultimate display of spiritual power. A captured enemy famed for his valor might even be given a bride the night before his torture as a sign of genuine respect. The first ordeal for such a captive consisted of running between two lines of women who struck him with clubs and thorny branches. If the warrior somehow managed to reach the end of the line without falling, he was immediately set free. This rarely occurred, as the victim usually fell to the ground and was beaten unconscious. Later he would be revived for the stake where he would be poked with burning torches and hot irons as he literally roasted to death. It was at this point that pieces of flesh might be cut away and eaten so that his captors could gain the warrior's *orenda.* Every effort was made to prolong the suffering but eventually the village leaders ate the heart and brains of the warrior while the remainder of the body and blood was distributed to the rest of the villagers.

The Iroquois raids upon one another during this period amounted to national suicide as the five nations physically murdered themselves in never-ending cycles of violence. The wise men of the tribes tried to bring about harmonious living by teaching about Teharonhiawagon, but it was not until the appearance of a young orator named Hiawatha that things began to change. Hiawatha was so filled with the teaching of the Master of Life that he felt he must travel to every Iroquois village to preach the virtues of peace. His first trips were along the Hudson River where he spoke to any council that would hear him. He soon met Deganawidah, a philosopher whose political ideas were the practical extension of Hiawatha's religious beliefs. Deganawidah had a speech impediment which made it impossible for him to spread his views among the eloquent Iroquois, but Hiawatha had the golden tongue of a prophet. He presented their combined ideas throughout the nations. The first conversions came in front of small village fires. This led to acceptance by clans until finally the Oneida became the first large nation to agree to cease warring on others if the others would do the same. The Cayuga, Seneca, and Mohawk quickly adhered to the Great Peace on the same condition. The powerful Onondaga were the last to agree and had to be given the honor of being Firekeeper of the proposed new government. Being Firekeeper meant they would be chairmen at all the councils and that the Great Council would always be held on Onondaga territory.

In later times the achievements of Hiawatha would become clouded by legends. Even white school children would memorize poems about him, but the Hiawatha they learned about was mistakenly placed in the Great Lakes region and his ideas were the projections of the white poet Henry Wadsworth Longfellow rather than the wisdom of the Iroquois. Some scholars would say Hiawatha had never existed and that the deeds ascribed to him had been done by several men. However many interpretations there might be, one thing was certain: the Great Peace was established by the formation of the League of the Five Nations. Its members vowed that they would never again fight other members. They would never again eat human flesh except as a symbolic act in wartime. Then braves would be allowed to taste the heart and brain of their enemies in order to gain their *orenda*. All old blood feuds were ended forever. All new disagreements would be submitted to the Great Council. The code of the confederation proclaimed the Great Peace in this graceful Iroquois phrasing:

> I, Deganawidah, and the Confederated chiefs, now uproot the tallest pine tree, and into the cavity thereby made we cast all weapons of war. Into the depths of the earth, down into the deep underearth currents of water flowing to unknown regions, we cast all weapons of war. We bury them from sight forever and plant again the Tree.

The League brought peace only to the Iroquois, but the Great Peace of Teharonhiawagon was a universal teaching meant for all nations. Soon, Iroquois orators were visiting other tribes to spread their ideas. Some groups gave nominal allegiance to the League through tokens of affiliation or by being adopted by Iroquois families and clans. In 1711 the Tuscarora would be driven from the South by the Europeans and would join the confederation to make it the League of the Six Nations.

The League sought peace but even an advanced thinker like Deganawidah approved of conversion by the sword. Thus, the fierce war spirit which made the Iroquois justly feared as warriors reasserted itself dramatically. At certain periods in the history of the League, the confederation became a multinational alliance commanding armies of thousands inspired both by religious crusading fervor and the desire for material gain.

The cruelty of the Iroquois was often commented on, but the very colonists who were shocked by Iroquois warfare put their own people in stocks, branded them, pierced their cheeks, cropped their ears, and burned "witches." The Europeans, unlike the Indians, had long made it a practice to slaughter one another over religious ideas. Nor was it unusual for the Europeans to use religion as an excuse for provoking wars with their business rivals. The

Europeans who called the Iroquois uncivilized did not allow their women to vote or to own property, and they thought it quite proper to sail thousands of miles to buy and sell human beings as slaves.

The English-speaking colonists had no sooner killed off the coastal Indians than they began to challenge the Iroquois. The Susquehanna of the South would not ally with the League against the whites because the Dutch and Spanish speakers had given them cannon and promised to build them forts. The Huron to the west were allies with the French speakers who had created a chain of forts and trading posts throughout the Great Lakes. Game grew scarcer and soon the Iroquois had nothing to trade. Without the gunpowder and tools of the whites, the Iroquois would be helpless. The League grew desperate. Once more runners were sent to their relations, the Huron, asking for furs, but once more the reply was no. The Mohawk grew especially angry because the whites were directly on their borders, and they suggested a new kind of war. The council fires burned many nights before the League reached a decision that changed all previous ideas about how to deal with rival nations.

The new League plan concerned the Huron who controlled the Great Lakes through a system of forced alliances. The Huron lived in stockades and had grown so wealthy they only hunted for pleasure. Their government was not so well organized as that of the Iroquois but the Hurons could mobilize war parties quickly and traders found it wiser to pay them a fee when passing through their territories than to risk a fight. The Huron had grown so confident of their power that they no longer fortified their cities and grew careless about defense in general. They had given up farming entirely, relying upon the

fifteen thousand Tobacco Huron to send them tribute in
the form of corn, beans, tobacco, and sunflower seeds.

The Iroquois had become jealous and bitter toward
their relatives. The survival of their nations was at stake.
When the Firekeeper pronounced the final decisions of
the Great Council to make war on the Huron, the power
committed was something never before dreamed of in
the woodlands. The decision for this war involved a revolution in Indian thinking. War had always been a private
rather than a political matter. War had been a matter of
a few men going out on a raid. Fighting went on all the
time but few basic political or economic changes ever
resulted. Only on rare occasions did one tribe or another
drive a rival from some hunting or planting ground. The
war the Iroquois now planned was new for Indians, a
European-style war.

An army of almost a thousand braves was sent to kill or
bring into the League all tribes engaged in the fur trade.
The first attack on the Huron took four hundred lives,
mostly women and children. The shock to the Huron was
mortal. The unthinkable had been done. The war party
had attacked through deep snows with an intensity of
purpose and thoroughness that the comfortable world of
the Huron could not understand. The Huron collapse was
as irrational as it was total: instead of rallying their warriors and seeking allies, the Huron panicked. They fled
from their villages as from a plague. Thousands were so
terrified they took refuge on a barren island where they
died from starvation. Over five hundred fled to Quebec
to seek the protection of the French. Others went to the
Neutral Indians who killed them now that Huron power
was shattering. A few found refuge with the Erie tribe
but in one year the all powerful Huron were reduced to

skeletons, ashes, and beggars. The Tobacco Huron survived by moving westward as the Iroquois relentlessly consolidated their victory. Huron power perished by 1649. The Neutrals gave in during the next two years, the Pennsylvania Susquehanna in 1653, and the Erie in 1654. The League reigned unchallenged for a generation and remained a dominant power for another eighty years after that. From the Great Lakes to the gray Atlantic and as far south as the Ohio River, Iroquois power was supreme. Some years not a single canoe-load of furs reached Montreal. The Iroquois used everything for trade with the British.

League diplomats played off the European powers against one another but they usually preferred dealing with the British who gave them better terms. Even so, the League became alarmed by the growth of the English-speaking settlements. They knew the coastal Algonkin people had been destroyed in spite of their friendship for the European newcomers. The League hoped to save themselves by leading a united defense against the whites. League diplomats spoke with the Creek: "Take care that you oblige all such as you make a peace with that they immediately remove and settle near to oppose your enemies . . . This is the method we take and we would have you do the same." The League proposed a plan for red solidarity. The League would act as the economic and military head of a confederation which all tribes could join as equals. The Creek were too confident of their own strength to agree. Most of the tribes beyond the Appalachians thought little of the danger of the new white tribes and were not interested in being drawn into faraway Iroquois intrigues. Others were allies with the French, whom they looked upon as benefactors.

Fighting along the westward-moving frontier was continuous, but the major conflicts were given names by the ever victorious whites: King Philip's War (1675), King William's War (1689–97), Queen Anne's War (1701–13), King George's War (1744–48), and the French and Indian War (1754–63). The Iroquois fought in some of the wars, but they warned tribes not to fight against the English in the French and Indian War which was the American part of the world-wide Seven Years' War between France and England. The grateful English rewarded the League for its decision with gifts presented by an extraordinary man named William Johnson who had been appointed to head Indian affairs in 1746. Sir William had wed a Mohawk woman and had her brother, Joseph Brant, educated at American and British schools. Johnson learned the Mohawk tongue and built a castle of wood logs on the Mohawk River in upper New York. His influence in the League was immense and intertribal bickering ended. Under his direction, the League expanded to eleven nations and its people lived comfortably in log houses with fireplaces, orchards, and gardens. Indian wealth upset the white settlers, and the Indians resented each new white expansion, but Sir William preserved an uneasy peace. Like the Huron before them, the Iroquois seemed secure in their strength and prosperity.

Iroquois power hinged upon the unity of the League. Two hundred years had passed since the time of Hiawatha. Iroquois tribes had fought separately but never against one another. Most economic and political problems had been solved when the outbreak of the American Revolution brought a new challenge. Sir William and Joseph Brant backed the British Crown and their view prevailed among the Mohawk, Seneca, Cayuga, and Onondaga;

Joseph Brant, a Mohawk leader who was educated in British schools, helped to convince most of the Iroquois to fight on the British side during the American Revolution. (*Courtesy of Museum of the American Indian, Heye Foundation*)

but local interests, jealousies, and distrust of the redcoats led the Oneida and Tuscarora to support the revolutionary colonists. Other allied nations thought the best path was neutrality. The debates in the councils were long and bitter. The Firekeeper patiently presented the various viewpoints again and again, yet the matter was beyond compromise. The tribes were still divided when the council fires were extinguished, but few understood the full extent of the disaster about to befall them.

English officers and revolutionaries seemed to fight harder against the Iroquois than against each other. One revolutionary army alone burned down forty villages and destroyed one hundred and sixty thousand bushels of corn. The merciless destruction continued for over six years and when the British finally granted independence to the colonists, there was little concern for the ruined Iroquois. Sir William died early in the war and Brant retreated with his followers to Canada. Some Iroquois moved west. Those who remained behind in the ashes of their greatness had to resist vigorous settlers who now controlled their own destiny and moved westward with an incredible hunger for land.

One of the banners of the victorious colonists showed a snake divided into thirteen segments with the inscription—Join or Die. Just when the thirteen council fires of the colonies united, the League divided. This fatal disunity meant the end of Iroquois freedom and the beginning of reservations. Spokesmen such as Red Jacket would be left to lament, "Our seats were once large and yours were very small. You have now become a great people and we have scarcely got a place left to spread our blankets." The power of the rattlesnake people had become divided

and thus it perished beneath the claws of the young eagle.
An old Iroquois song took on new meaning:

> Now no sun is shining.
> Now no star is glowing.
> Come show us the pathway.
> The night is not friendly.
> She closes her eyelids.
> The moon has forgotten us.
> We wait in the darkness.

PONTIAC'S GREAT WAR

Nations related to the Iroquois by similar languages lived
to the west of the Iroquois around the Great Lakes and
nearby rivers. Life in the region was pleasant. Forests of
birch, conifers, beech, oak, elm, and chestnut trees provided shelter in summer. Fields of oats and wild rice were
gifts of the good manitous (spirits). Winters were harsh
at times but buckskin clothing and sturdy wooden lodges
allowed the moons of mist and snow to pass without
disaster. Villages of elm houses stretched for miles along
streams and rivers with hundreds of canoes pulled up
along the shore. The tribesmen often went nude in summer while the women preferred pretty skirts. Both sexes
took pride in their good looks and in their luxuriant black
hair which rarely turned gray. Men cut their hair close on
either side of their head, leaving a cockscomb from forehead to the back of the neck. Decorated with shells, metal,
and other ornaments the men looked like plumed
knights and, like plumed knights, they spent most of their

time in romance and war. Lovers wooed one another with music and poetry. A few phrases broken by passages on a flute, rattles, or just humming gave their songs an entrancing quality.

War was a matter of individual fame-seeking. Opponents who preferred death to capture were granted their wish and torture was rare. Scalp taking was not considered important. What was crucial was that a man do something outstanding to increase his reputation or earn himself a new name. The farther west the tribe was located the more it tended to adopt the custom of the plains Indians who deemed it more courageous to touch a living warrior with a ceremonial stick than to kill him from a distance. Feats of valor were acted out before the campfire in a drama of dance and song. No one could falsify on such occasions as the other warriors permitted no exaggerations. The chief of a war party was usually an individual who had power only in time of trouble while a peace chief, chosen for his wisdom, held office for life and was the leader of village affairs. The home of the peace chief was a sanctuary for wrongdoers and even a sacrificial dog might escape his doom by taking refuge there. Some chiefs trying to preserve the peace went so far as to have themselves tied up in order to elicit pity from the quarreling parties. If all compromises failed, a few warriors put red pigment on their temples and cheeks and black around their eyes and forehead as a sign they were at war. These painted war masks had no special pattern. Each man was expected to use his imagination to create the most frightening design possible.

The tribes were referred to as the people of the calumet because of the immense respect they placed in what the whites called pipes. These ornamental objects were long,

Hunters and fishermen in the Great Lakes area liked to go out in the early morning. (*Huntington Free Library, Heye Foundation*)

elaborate stems which usually but not always had a pipe bowl at the end. They were skillfully decorated with rare feathers, carvings, beading, and quill work. The calumets had a variety of ceremonial and political uses. Being given a calumet guaranteed an individual safe conduct through a war zone and served as identification and protection far more effectively than the modern system of passports and visas.

The people of the calumet generally preferred the French to the English, for the French settlements tended to remain small trading centers that did not expand. Most of the tribes rallied to the French side during the French and Indian War. From the famous defeat of General Braddock's and Colonel Washington's troops in Pennsylvania to skirmishes throughout the Great Lakes, the Indians never tasted defeat on the battlefield. When envoys carrying sacred calumets brought the news that a French defeat in the distant city of Quebec meant the English would occupy the forts they had never won in battle, the Indians were astounded. English racist policies soon turned this initial astonishment into outrage and a new war.

The new British Commander in Chief was Sir Jeffrey Amherst, a man who hated the Indians and regarded them as racial inferiors. One of his first orders was to end the French practice of giving free food, ammunition, and other gifts to Indians who stopped at forts. Amherst forbade private traders to sell liquor to Indians and when the order was disobeyed, he restricted trading of all kinds to the forts. The English had never defeated the Indians, yet they were acting like conquerors. The French gifts had been valuable to the Indians, especially during difficult winters. The traders who came to Indian villages meant that Indians were spared the dangers of the winter trail. The various fort commanders tried to keep knowledge of the new policy hidden for as long as possible in the vain hope that Amherst would change his mind.

The most powerful tribe in the area was the Ottawa, who had slowly taken up the place left by the defeat of the Huron and the gradual erosion of Iroquois strength. The chief leader of the Ottawa was Pontiac, a warrior whose rise was so swift that the whites never knew the exact reasons for his influence. The actions of the English so angered Pontiac that he called for a great council to be held in 1763. Hundreds of warriors representing the Potawatomi, Ottawa, and the last of the Huron responded. Pontiac inflamed the council by citing English insults and by flattering the braves with stories of their past victories. He said that just as a victory at Quebec had given the

English possession of Fort Detroit, so an Indian victory at Detroit would bring the French back into the war with the English. He spoke of a vision a Delaware prophet had told him about in which the Great Spirit had said:

> The land on which you live I have made for you, and not for others. Why do you suffer the white men to dwell among you? My children, you have forgotten the customs and traditions of your forefathers. Why do you not clothe yourselves in skins, as they did, and use the bows and arrows, and the stone-pointed lances, which they used? You have bought guns, knives, kettles, and blankets from the white men, until you can no longer do without them; and, what is worse, you have drunk the poison fire-water, which turns you all into fools. Fling all these things away; live as your wise forefathers lived before you. And as for these English—these dogs dressed in red, who have come to rob you of your hunting-grounds, and drive away the game —you must lift the hatchet against them. Wipe them from the face of the earth, and then you will win my favor back again and once more be happy and prosperous.

Pontiac's oratory inflamed the assembly and runners were sent out to various tribes asking them to rise against the English when called upon. An attempt to gain entrance to Fort Detroit by putting on a ball game for the amusement of the whites was ruined when the plan was revealed by an informer, most likely the Ottawa mistress of the fort's commander. Rather than giving up after this first failure, Pontiac made an alliance with the French settlers in the area. They gave him substantial aid in exchange for promises of repayment written on birch bark and stamped with the animal sign that was Pontiac's personal mark. The Ottawa had no artillery but Pontiac directed his men in an attack on the fortress. The garrison held back the Indians, but again rather than leave as Indians usually left after such a defeat, the Ottawa began a siege and Pontiac sent runners to his many allies telling them the hour had come for their war paint.

Bands of Chippewa, Potawatomi, Delaware, Mingo, Sauk, Seneca, Miami, Shawnee, Huron, and Ottawa responded to Pontiac's call with attacks throughout the Great Lakes area. Fort Sandusky, Fort Miami, Fort Ouiatenon, Fort Mackinac, Fort Joseph, Fort Venango, Fort Le Boeuf, and Fort Presque fell to the victorious Indians. Fort Edward Augustus on Green Bay was abandoned and English military units were defeated on Lake St. Clair, the Niagara River, and Lake Erie. The Monongahela Valley in Pennsylvania was devastated and Fort Pitt was put under siege. In a swift two months the English lost every one of their forts in the Great Lakes except for the besieged Fort Detroit and Fort Pitt. The supply lines across Lake Erie were weak and the one from Niagara to Pitt broken.

The Indian successes astounded Amherst, who immediately sent a relief column to Detroit with orders to seek out and destroy all Indians. An attack on Pontiac's forces turned the streams red with English blood and the defeated column retreated behind the walls of the fort. New groups of Indians now struck the entire frontier from New York to Virginia. Hundreds of settlers were killed in their cabins and thousands more fled back across the Appalachian Mountains. A relief force managed to break the siege at Fort Pitt but other reinforcements were wiped out in the vicinity of Niagara Falls.

The defeats humiliated the racist Amherst, who abandoned the gentlemen's rules used for dealing with white opponents such as the French in favor of open war crimes. His Detroit commander was told to kill all prisoners of war and his Pennsylvania commander was ordered to spread smallpox among the Indians through the use of infected blankets. Amherst described his foes as the "vilest race of beings that ever infested the earth" and he spoke of killing them all as self-righteously as if he were ridding mankind of the bubonic plague. He offered a hundred pounds to anyone who killed Pontiac and then a few weeks later doubled the bounty.

These desperate measures proved ineffective, but Pontiac had other problems. His patriotic speeches and the brilliant spring offensive could not change traditional habits of war. Braves who had been in victories wanted to return home to enjoy their booty and to celebrate their deeds with feasts and dancing. Those who were unsuccessfully besieging Detroit were unhappy at the lack of exploits to boast about. Pontiac was prepared to fight on with only his personal Ottawa followers if necessary when word came that the French would no longer support him. The French stated that if the Indians continued to fight, all the whites would unite against them. Pontiac attempted a final negotiation with the Detroit commander but his message was not answered. The sad chief reluctantly ended the siege.

Pontiac used the next year going from tribe to tribe in an effort to resurrect the alliance. Some of his former warriors agreed to fight again but most had joined forces with the French and would fight only if the English attacked them first. Pontiac tried to make alliances with tribes as far south as Florida and with tribes on the banks of the Father of Waters but he could get no firm pledges from anyone. His efforts were so unproductive that by the spring of 1765 he realized he could not renew the war. In April he contacted General Gage, the new British Commander in Chief, who promised to treat him as a worthy and honorable political leader. That August, Pontiac made a peace speech in which he said:

> I declare to all nations that I had settled my peace with you before I came here and now deliver my pipe to be sent to Sir William Johnson that he may know I have made peace and taken the King of England for my father, in the presence of all the nations now assembled; and whenever any of those nations go to visit him, they may smoke out of it with him in peace.

Gage was not completely satisfied because he feared Pontiac might change his mind. Rather than martyr or harm Pontiac, the British commander spread the rumor that the only reason Pontiac spoke for peace was because he had been placed on the British payroll. In 1768, Gage provided an elaborate escort to take Pontiac to see Sir William Johnson in New York. No effort was spared to make the other tribes and chiefs envious by treating Pontiac as a powerful European-style monarch rather than as a successful Indian general. The British cunning received its reward a year later when an unknown warrior literally stabbed Pontiac in the back while the chief was in Illinois. The leader who had shaken the frontier empire of the British died ingloriously on the floor of a white trading post.

TECUMSEH, THE WAITING PANTHER

The American Revolution was almost as disastrous for the Indians of the Great Lakes as it was for the League of the Five Nations. At first there was the excitement of a new war, with the English supplying ammunition and other gifts. Some warriors went to Montreal to participate in General Burgoyne's invasion of New York, and others joined the Iroquois of the Mohawk Valley. Once more the frontier blazed with Indian exploits, and once more the Indians had chosen the losing side and had to fight on alone. Their active resistance to the United States continued until 1794 when General "Mad" Anthony Wayne came into the area with a determined army. A large body of Indians waited for Wayne at a place called Fallen Timbers where a wind storm had cleared a place in the forest. The Indians fought well but were finally driven from the battlefield by a spirited charge of bluecoats with fixed bayonets. Among the defeated warriors was a young Shawnee called Tecumseh, the Waiting Panther. Tecumseh understood that the old Indian ways of organizing a war were inadequate against the power they had to face. The Shawnee knew how the French had abandoned Pontiac and he was not surprised when the British closed their forts to the survivors of Fallen Timbers.

Wayne's victory was a mortal threat to Indian life. One of the prime grievances of the colonists had been that the British had limited or halted settlement beyond the Appalachians. The new republic had no such policies and whites poured across the passes. Many long rifles moved into sparsely populated Kentucky and Tennessee. Thousands of Indians suddenly faced the prospect of removal or extermination. Individual tribes fought courageously, but one by one, the settlers eliminated them. Some chiefs were all too eager to sell their lands if properly bribed. Some sought honest compromises but found themselves betrayed. Only a united Indian nation led by patriotic and courageous chiefs could hold back the white influx. Should the tribes from the Great Lakes to the Gulf of Mexico unite

Tecumseh, the outstanding Shawnee war chief and orator, told the whites that Indian land was owned by all in common and was not to be sold: "Why not sell the air, the clouds, and the great sea as well as the earth?" (*Courtesy of Museum of the American Indian, Heye Foundation*)

under a federated leadership, they would have the strength to make meaningful alliances with the European powers instead of relying on the traditional haphazard handouts. Backed by their own might and European allies, the Indians would have a chance for survival. If they did not unite, the Indian star would surely set forever. The Waiting Panther understood the situation perfectly and proceeded to work for the creation of a new red nation.

Like Hiawatha before him, Tecumseh began to travel from village to village speaking of Indian nationhood. His most important early convert was his own one-eyed brother who had been an idler until he became affected by the religious fervor that shook the white frontier in 1805. He was particularly influenced by the Shakers who jerked and danced with psychic power in a fashion the red men understood and admired. The settlers called him the Prophet but he took the name Tenskwatawa, The Open Door, after the saying of Jesus, "I am the door." The two Shawnee brothers moved to Greenville in Ohio where the chiefs had formally surrendered to Wayne in 1795. Their challenge to the whites and traditional Indian leadership could not have been made clearer.

Religious problems plagued the brothers during their first months in their new camp. The Prophet was able to use an eclipse of the sun to build his reputation as a holy man but his converts often attacked Christian Indians and others who would not accept his teachings. Tecumseh spent much of his time halting this destructive in-fighting. The Indians had never fought about religion before and Tecumseh now taught that an individual's religion was a personal matter as long as the individual supported the ideal of Indian nationhood. Tecumseh patiently organized units of support in tribal councils as he sought to build a structure that would rise naturally from the people. He noted which chiefs were weak, money-hungry, or overly friendly to whites, and worked to remove them in favor of men loyal to his own leadership. When settlers moved close to his Greenville headquarters, Tecumseh recognized he was still too weak to fight and he moved his camp to an area on the Tippecanoe River which the Potawatomi and Kickapoo offered to him.

Almost fifty winters had passed since Pontiac's time. Now, Tecumseh proved to be an even more persuasive orator and organizer than his illustrious Ottawa predecessor. Tecumseh spoke to the councils of the northern tribes. Chiefs who had signed the peace treaties were removed from office in favor of more militant leadership. Groups of Potawatomi, Kickapoo, Delaware, Wyandot, Wea, Chippewa, and Illinois pledged their support of a new kind of alliance. In far-off Wisconsin, Black Hawk, an important leader among the Sauk and Fox, promised to fight whenever the Shawnee called for action. Only the Missisinewa and Miami, who remained under the influence of the compromising Little Turtle, resisted the power of his logic.

Feeling that his influence among the northern tribes was firm, Tecumseh spent most of 1809 traveling to distant nations. Always escorted by armed supporters, he journeyed as far south as Florida and as far west as the banks of the Missouri. Firm guarantees of co-operation were fewer and less definite, but Tecumseh was satisfied that he had created a real foundation for future action. He had established himself as the symbol of Indian unity and absolute defiance of the whites. Everywhere the young warriors worshiped him. Governor Harrison of the Northwest Territory voiced the sentiment of many in recognizing his uniqueness when he described Tecumseh as:

. . . one of those uncommon geniuses, which spring up occasionally to produce revolutions and overturn the established order of things. If it were not for the vicinity of the United States, he would perhaps be the founder of an Empire that would rival in glory that of Mexico or Peru.

Head men such as Little Turtle continued to make agreements with the Americans. Alcohol, defeatism, bribes, and other pressures led these leaders to cede three million acres in Indiana. Much of the territory was occupied by peoples not even represented by the signing chiefs, and the ceded land included the best of the Shawnee hunting grounds. The agreement brought Tecumseh to a fighting rage. He declared that Indian country was not the property of any one person or any one tribe. The new treaties were treason and all the men of Waiting Panther would die before giving up an inch to the United States. A thousand warriors responded to his call to rally at the Prophet's town on the Tippecanoe.

Governor Harrison had long wanted to meet with the Shawnee brothers and the fresh challenge prompted him to call for a conference. On August 11, 1810, Tecumseh and the Prophet arrived at Harrison's camp on the Wabash River escorted by hundreds of armed warriors. Harrison had been under the impression that the Prophet was the major leader of the Indians, but Tecumseh's brilliant oratory soon removed any doubt as to who was in charge. The Waiting Panther praised the heroic chiefs of the coastal people and exposed the treacherous record of broken white promises. He spoke boldly of his plan of a united Indian confederation:

Since my residence at Tippecanoe, we have endeavored to level all distinctions, to destroy village chiefs, by whom all mischiefs are done. It is they who sell the land to the Americans. Brother, this land that was sold, and the goods that were given for it, was only done by a few . . . In the future we are prepared to punish those who propose to sell land to the Americans. If you continue to purchase them, it will make war among the different tribes, and, at last, I do not know what will be the consequences among the white people . . . If you will not give up the land and do cross the boundary of our present settlement, it will be very hard, and produce trouble between us.

The way, the only way, to stop this evil is for the red men to unite in claiming a common and equal right in the land, as it was at first, and should be now—for it was never divided, but belongs to all. No tribe has the right to sell, even to each other, much less to strangers who demand all and will settle for no less . . . Sell a country! Why not sell the air, the clouds, and the great sea as well as the earth? Did not the Great Spirit make them all for the use of his children?

How can we have confidence in the white people? When Jesus Christ came upon the earth you killed Him and nailed Him to a cross . . .

The states have set the example of forming a union among all their fires—why should they censure us for following it?

Harrison was badly shaken by the audacity and rationality of Tecumseh's presentation. The chief interrupted the governor whenever Harrison tried to avoid or refute the thesis of common ownership of the land. Tempers soared and a fight was averted when Harrison abruptly ended the meeting. The two leaders met the following day and talked while sitting on a bench. Tecumseh began to nudge closer to Harrison, who moved toward the edge to avoid an argument. At last the governor objected that he was about to be shoved off entirely. Tecumseh laughed and said that now perhaps Harrison could understand what the Indians felt. The conference continued for the rest of the day but nothing could be resolved.

When a group of Potawatomi killed a number of whites the following summer, Harrison demanded that Tecumseh and the Prophet give up. The Shawnees refused and the governor used the incident to stir up the settlers. Fearing that the tribes in the South and West might still hold back in case of war, Tecumseh launched a new organizing effort. Harrison noted his departure and informed his superiors in Washington that he hoped to destroy the northern alliance before Tecumseh returned.

Councils numbering in the thousands came to listen to Tecumseh as he visited every Indian nation in the South. Observers spoke of his pride and fervor. They reported that his intense call for unity inspired the young as no leader had ever inspired them before. The Creek and Seminole gave their oaths to rise as nations and although others did not follow their example, Tecumseh dreamed that a few more trips might be sufficient to complete his design. The old chiefs might still balk at his message but again and again the young braves shouted their allegiance to the new ideal. Even the Choctaw and Chickasaw of the South who did not favor alliance might be made to understand with time:

> The whites are already nearly a match for us all united, and too strong for any one tribe alone to resist; so that unless we support one another with our collective and united forces; unless every tribe unanimously combines to give check to the ambition and avarice of the whites, they will soon conquer us apart and disunited . . . Where today is the Pequod? Where the Narragansett? The Mohican? The Pocanoket? And many other once powerful tribes of our race? They have vanished before the avarice and oppression of the white men as snow before a summer sun . . . Think not, brave Choctaws and Chickasaws, that you can remain passive and indifferent to the common danger, and thus escape the common fate . . . You, too, will

be driven away from your native land and ancient domains as leaves are driven before the wintry storms. Sleep not longer, O Choctaws and Chickasaws, in false security and delusive hopes.

The shrewd Harrison knew better than to let the Shawnee have time to complete his work of persuasion and alliance building. The governor moved an army up the Wabash River and made a fortified camp near the Prophet's town. Although Tecumseh had specifically warned his brother not to fight with the whites in his absence, the Prophet agreed with a Winnebago group that wanted to begin the battle at dawn. The Prophet sent his men to battle with the following rallying cry:

> O Shawnee braves! O Potawatomi men! O Miami Panthers! O Ottawa Foxes! O Miami Lynxes! O Kickapoo Beavers! O Winnebago Wolves! Lift up your hatchets; raise your knives; sight your rifles! Have no fears—your lives are charmed! Stand up to the foe; he is a weakling and a coward! O red brothers, fall upon him! Wound, rend, tear, and flay, scalp, and leave him to the wolves and buzzards! O Shawnee braves! O Potawatomi men!

Never before and never again would Indians engage in such a pitched battle as they did that day on the Tippecanoe. Tecumseh had trained them well in the white man's tactics, but Harrison's men stood their ground and without Tecumseh's generalship, the Indians were not able to break the bluecoat defense. By nightfall, the Indians retreated and the next day the Prophet's town was burned to the ground. Afterward, Harrison boasted of his victory everywhere and the luster of the triumph was enough eventually to carry him to the presidency of the United States.

Tecumseh was enraged by the disaster his brother's impatience had caused. The military loss was minor but the image of an invincible union had been broken. He nearly

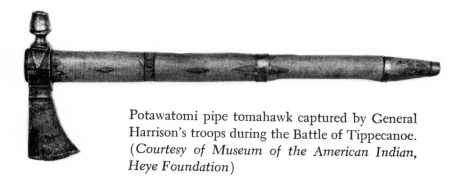

Potawatomi pipe tomahawk captured by General Harrison's troops during the Battle of Tippecanoe. (*Courtesy of Museum of the American Indian, Heye Foundation*)

killed his brother from anger before chasing him away. The Prophet wandered without followers throughout the West and was never again a leader. Uprisings of the kind Tecumseh feared would upset his plan flared everywhere. Angry groups of Indians in Illinois and Indiana tried to avenge the defeat at Tippecanoe. They fought without a general strategy and they were unable to follow up their initial successes. Most tribes waited for Tecumseh's personal command. Others pulled away entirely, fearing they would be drawn into a hopeless war. The fighting was the beginning of the end of Tecumseh's vision, but he understood the outrage of his countrymen. Later, he would speak of his indignation and humiliation upon finding the Prophet's town in ashes:

> My mission to my mother's land had failed. I could not induce them to come where the water turns to stone and the rain comes from the clouds in showers of white wool to bury everything in sight. I had to shut my eyes all the way so as not to see the beautiful country that would soon be trampled under the feet of the hated white men . . . I stood upon the ashes of my home, where my own wigwam had sent up its fires to the Great Spirit; where I summoned the spirits of the braves who had fallen in their vain attempt to protect their homes from the grasping invaders. And as I sniffed up the smell of their blood from the earth, I swore eternal hatred—the hatred of the avenger.

Most people in the border states blamed the Indian uprisings entirely upon the outside agitation of the British. This sentiment was a major force in bringing on the War of 1812. Anxious to keep as many Indians as possible from fighting for the British, the United States called a council at Fort Wayne to give gifts and make new promises. Tecumseh attended the meeting and thundered his defiance of the United States. He said that if the British won the war, they might grant some land to the Indians, but if the United States won, there was no hope. He said the bluecoats planned to drive every tribe toward the setting sun until one day they would drown the last Indian in the ocean beyond the western mountains. Tecumseh's body shook with hostility and pride as he snapped the peace pipes. The assembly responded to him as to their own soul.

Black Hawk brought braves from as far away as Wisconsin and even Sioux from the edge of the Plains came to join the struggle. English and Indian runners carried the word that Waiting Panther was on the war path. So many warriors responded that Tecumseh understood anew how near he had been to success. The tribes fought brilliantly but the war was not the all-Indian affair Tecumseh had envisioned. Red men did not fight for specific Indian goals under a unified group of leaders. Nonetheless they arose on every front and on every front they drove out the whites. Not a single white was safe in the Great Lakes, Upper Mississippi, or the Deep South. Tecumseh himself helped capture Fort Detroit, the victory that had eluded even Pontiac. After a trip by Tecumseh to the South, which no white man was allowed to observe, the Creek rose up in the most widespread war ever fought in that region.

The war went well on all Indian fronts, but Tecumseh knew the end result would be no different than earlier wars.

He knew the British would betray the Indians whenever it suited their interests. He tried to unite the fighting tribes, but what had been difficult in peace was impossible in war. Indian victories remained separate acts of courage and individual daring. The Indian nation was not to be. A despondent Tecumseh began to place himself at the head of battle and to take unnecessary risks. At the Battle of the Thames while commanding both British soldiers and Indian warriors, a stray bullet brought an end to his life and the last fading possibility of an Indian alliance east of the Mississippi River.

FAREWELL, MY NATION

The establishment of the United States did not mean the Indian nations must automatically perish. In the beginning the attitude in the United States was that Indians were sovereign people organized in nations entitled to govern themselves. In 1789 Congress decreed:

> The utmost good faith shall always be observed towards the Indians, their land and personal property shall never be taken from them without their consent and in their property, rights, and liberty they shall never be invaded or disturbed, unless in just and lawful wars . . .

Thomas Jefferson admired the Indians. He remarked that hearing them speak filled him with awe and envy. Had a powerful Indian confederation with some natural physical defenses such as lakes and mountains come into being under the leadership of patriots with the skills of Pontiac and Tecumseh, liberals such as Jefferson would have been prone to bargain honorably. What destroyed Indian chances for survival was not so much the military power of the whites as their ruthless racial bigotry which poisoned too much of the American bloodstream. Senator John C. Calhoun, a spokesman for black slavery and one of the most powerful men in the United States Senate, expressed what came to be the majority view in the United States, "The Indians are not in fact an independent people, nor ought they be so considered. They should be taken under our guardianship, and our opinions, and not theirs ought to prevail, in measures intended for their civilization and happiness." Calhoun's sophisticated prejudice was an extension of the exterminating spirit that had moved Pilgrim William Bradford to celebrate a 1638 massacre of the Indians with these words:

> Those that escaped ye fire were slain with ye sword . . . It is conceded they thus destroyed about four hundred. It was a fearful sight to see them thus frying in ye fyer . . . but ye victory seemed a sweete sacrifice and they gave prays thereof to God.

Civilization and Christianity were convenient banners the Bradfords and Calhouns held up to excuse their greed and racism. After the War of 1812, it was obvious the United States would reach the banks of the Mississippi. Most Indians chose to fight hopeless wars rather than suffer the dishonor of cowardly surrender. None was more militant than Black Hawk, the implacable follower of Tecumseh, who fought a brief yet spectacular war in Wisconsin. Upon his surrender he delivered an oration which transcended personal grievances to depict the clash of civilizations. Black Hawk was prepared to die for the old ways, not because he was stubborn or stupid, but because he did not wish to become like the white men:

Black Hawk has done nothing for which an Indian ought to be ashamed. He has fought for his countrymen, against the white men who came, year after year, to cheat them and take away their lands. You know the cause of our making war. It is known to all white men. They ought to be ashamed of it. The white men despise the Indians and drive them back from their homes. But the Indians are not deceitful. The white men speak bad of the Indian and look at him spitefully. But the Indian does not tell lies. Indians do not steal. An Indian who is as bad as a white man could not live in our nation. He would be put to death and eaten by the wolves.

The white men are bad schoolmasters. They carry false looks and deal in false actions. They smile in the face of the poor Indian, to cheat him; they shake him by the hand to gain his confidence, to make him drunk, and to deceive him. We told them to let us alone, and keep away from us; but they followed and beset our paths, and they coiled themselves among us, like the snake. They poisoned us by their touch. We were not safe; we lived in danger. We were becoming like them, hypocrites and liars; all talkers and no workers.

. . . The white men do not scalp the head, they do worse—they poison the heart. It is not pure with them. His countrymen will not be scalped but will in a few years be like the white men, so you cannot trust them; and there must be as in the white settlements as many officers as men, to take care of them, and keep them in order.

Farewell, my nation! Black Hawk tried to save you and avenge your wrongs. He drank the blood of some of the whites. He has been taken prisoner, and his plans are stopped. He can do no more! He is near his end. His sun is setting and he will rise no more. Farewell to Black Hawk!

Sequoya invented an eighty-five letter alphabet to record every sound of the Cherokee language. (*Courtesy of Museum of the American Indian, Heye Foundation*)

PART II

As Long as the Grass Shall Grow: The Southeast

Our hatchets are broken, our bows are snapped, our fires extinguished . . . a little longer and the white man will cease to persecute us for we shall cease to exist.

The Prophet (Creek)

Southeastern Tribes

WOODLANDS OF THE SOUTH

The forest stretched eastward from the Father of Waters to the gray Atlantic. The Indians who lived there could have survived just by gathering the fruit, roots, and vegetables growing wild, but they were skillful farmers with cultivated orchards and fields of corn. They lived in permanent villages with the head man's hut at one end of the square and the council house at the other. They dressed according to the weather, which might mean going naked in summer and using fur robes during a bad winter. They spent a lot of energy teasing their hair into various pompadour styles and decorated it with all manner of ornaments and feathers. The intelligence and confidence of the Creek, Choctaw, Chickasaw, Cherokee, and Seminole were so impressive that the whites called them the Five Civilized Tribes.

Each village council was led by a chief who held his post by virtue of ability and wisdom rather than birth. A common language, customs, marital ties, and religious views united a town or group of towns. Central government never developed although there were several sizable informal confederations, especially among the Creek. Often a special sub-chief would lead a town when there was a war or a feud to be fought. Certain families gained prestige and their members tended to have an advantage when a head man was selected, but the system was essentially democratic. Each village was independent and no head man could make any decision without consulting his council. No action could be undertaken without fasting and seeking the wisdom of the medicine men even if the matter were an athletic contest with another town. Decisions always involved the oldsters, the Beloved Men, and those who had spiritual and military power, the Big Warriors. Some villages were called red towns because of their association with aggression and their excellent warriors. White towns, on the other hand, were places of refuge and sanctuary and were associated with peaceful pursuits. Self-government was very real to the Southeasterners. When Tecumseh came to stir them to war against the United States, Pushmataha, a Choctaw chief, criticized the Shawnee for being undemocratic:

> Every Shawnee man, woman, and child must bow in humble submission to your imperious will. The Choctaws and Chickasaws have no monarchs. Their chieftains do not undertake the mastery of their people, but rather they are the people's servants, elected to serve the will of the majority.

The Choctaw and Chickasaw voted against Tecumseh, but they were hardly strangers to the war path. War was the way to manhood among all the five nations. Until a man had killed and scalped, he had to keep his child's name and suffer the humiliation of being teased beside the campfire. A glorious war deed brought dignity, a new name, and possibly a prized tattoo. The Cherokee said, "We cannot live without war. Should we make peace with the Tuscarora, we must immediately look for another nation with whom we can be engaged in our beloved occupation." But this beloved occupation was not like the political war of Europeans.

Southeastern war consisted of surprise raids by small commando parties. The warriors often followed in each other's footsteps to conceal their numbers. A "magic bundle" containing various good luck charms was kept pointed in the direction of the enemy. When the camp of the foe was reached, the attack was swift, with the raiders taking parts of bodies as well as scalps. Any prisoners were taken back to the attacking village. Men would be tortured in much the way the Iroquois tortured their captives, while women and children were usually adopted or enslaved. In spite of the fierceness and importance of this raiding, it was more personal than national. Indians spoke of blood feuds lasting hundreds of years, but these were between specific tribelets and clans. They did not interfere with common games, trading, feasting, and alliances against third parties.

War was the beloved occupation and torture was one of its components, but village life was essentially peaceful and pleasant. Harming a fellow villager was a serious matter, and murder was the one crime for which there was no forgiveness. Early settlers mistook dignified Indian diplomacy and respect for strangers as a personality trait. They did not know how fond the Indians were of gossiping, playing, and joking. Children were rarely punished, a white practice the Indians did not approve of or understand. Group farming and group hunting eliminated inequality in wealth and the possibilities of exploitation. Women did not have the prestige or power that Iroquois women had, but their lives were not especially difficult. Marriage was through the female clan, and there was considerable respect for menstruation and pregnancy. Divorce was a simple matter, and there was trial marriage without reprisals in case of failure. Feasts and games were a large part of life. Bear ribs, corn bread, and persimmon wine were only a few of the good things to be found in most villages. Southeastern lives tended to find natural pathways just as modern engineers have discovered their trails followed the natural contours of the earth. Pushmataha said, "We have grown up as the herbs in the woods."

The one place where the harsh war spirit became part of everyday life was in the education of young men. The Creek forced their children to bathe every morning, even if the creeks were iced over. They scratched young boys with fish bones so that future warriors would not be afraid of pain or blood. They were not fanatical, however, and if a particular youth did not wish to be a warrior, he could wear women's clothes and do women's work. He was not criticized for this, but he could never earn the prized tattoos or sing a war song such as this one from the Cherokee:

Careful: my knife drills your soul
              listen, whatever-your-name-is
              One of the wolf people
listen   I'll grind your saliva into the earth
listen   I'll cover your bones with black flint
listen   I'll cover your bones with black feathers
listen   I'll cover your bones with rocks
Because you're going where it's empty . . .

The Great Corn Dance or Busk held in July and August dealt with far more pleasant feelings and was open to everyone in society. This event was the major religious holiday of the region. The Seminole regarded it as the beginning of the new year. At this time, every crime except murder was forgiven. The Seminole had many customs involving fire, for like most Indians they related fire to the power of the sun. Fire could make an arrow wound safe. Fire kept one warm when there was frost. Fire was pure and made food good to eat. During the days of the Busk, shamans prepared new communal fires and every woman obtained purified flames for her own home. Houses were swept clean. Group baths were taken. Old dishes were smashed. Every step was taken to insure as pure a rededication to life as possible. On the third day of the celebration, all the adult men fasted and drank a liquid made of shrub leaves called the black drink. This tealike liquid gave them diarrhea and made them vomit in yet another effort to purge all unclean thoughts and deeds from the village. The celebration was crowned by an impressive feast of corn and roasted deer followed by a lively variety of games, songs, and dancing, each new joy binding the nation into a harmonious unity.

The Spanish were the first Europeans to enter the South. They landed in Florida in 1565. The British established the colony of South Carolina in 1673 and the French sailed into Mobile Bay in 1679. Each of these nations wanted to do business with the Indians and to use them against other Europeans. The Indians soon found themselves constantly at war, sometimes allied with one power, sometimes with another. The tribes survived and even prospered in this political situation, yet older chiefs warned that it was not good. When the United States came into being in 1789, its politicians began to speak of the republic's "manifest destiny" to spread from ocean to ocean. Such transcontinental dreams could only be realized at the expense of Indian civilization.

Following the end of the War of 1812, settlers from the United States rushed into the region occupied by the Five Nations. One of the immediate goals of the eagle's claw was Spanish Florida, and the Creek stood directly in the line of advance. At the Battle of Horseshoe Bend in 1814, Andrew Jackson broke the military power of the Creek and

Sequoya's alphabet spread throughout the Cherokee nation and soon there were newspapers, documents, and shop signs in Cherokee letters. (*Courtesy of Museum of the American Indian, Heye Foundation*)

made them give up most of their land. By 1817 the high-handed Jackson was making illegal raids into Florida. Less than two years later, the Spanish sold the peninsula for five million dollars rather than fight wars they could not possibly win. Conferences with the Indians followed. The United States made many new promises. Speckled Snake, an aging Creek chief, saw beneath the gifts and words: "I have listened to a great many talks from our Great Father. But they always began and ended in this—Get a little farther, you are too near me."

The Choctaw and other tribes who had aided Andrew Jackson against the Creek expected to be treated differently. They had adopted many of the ways of the Europeans and considered themselves a part of the young republic. After all, their fathers had campaigned with George Washington. When Lafayette, the most famous of the Europeans who had fought for the American Revolution, made a trip to the United States in 1825, Pushmataha thought it normal to take some people to meet him:

> Nearly fifty snows have melted since you drew your sword as a champion of Washington . . . You see everywhere the children of those by whose side you went to battle, crowding around you and shaking your hand as the hand of a father. We have heard these things told us in our villages, and our hearts longed to see you. We have come. We have taken you by the hand and we are satisfied. This is the first time we have seen you; it will probably be the last. We have no more to say: the earth will part us forever.

The tribes who had been enemies of the United States were just as eager as the Choctaw to be friends of the republic. The Creek, in particular, did everything in their power to heal old hatreds. An extraordinary Cherokee named Sequoya, who had been crippled while hunting, saw the need for a written language. Although his council elders ridiculed him for wanting to make "talking leaf" symbols like the whites, Sequoya went ahead with creating an alphabet. In 1821 he was able to present eighty-five characters that contained every sound in the Cherokee language. His people hailed him as a national hero and within a few short years everyone was reading and writing. Newspapers were printed in Cherokee, and men of the council corresponded with European nations and powerful politicians in Washington. Eventually, a national constitution

very much like that of the United States was written and
adopted. This phenomenal development was just another
indication of Indian vitality. If any of the nations could
have become assimilated peacefully into the new system,
the people of the Southeast were those people. Some had
been allies of George Washington. All wanted to co-oper-
ate. They had been open to change whenever change
meant a better way of living, but they were also proud
nations who desired to keep many of their traditional
ways. The American ark had no place for such a people.

The troubles always revolved around land. Always the
United States wanted just a little more. Always it promised that this would be the last time. The new promise was
to move the tribes to a land beyond the Father of Waters
where no white man would ever venture. The idea seemed
reasonable to whites, but when Chief MacIntosh of the
Creek signed such an agreement, his tribe executed him
for treason. Cherokee petitions were sent to the Congress
and President asking if the Indians were going to be
hunted like wild beasts. There was no official reply other
than the sounds of bluecoats marching in the woodlands.
Some bands retreated to the mountains and after years of
fighting gained small reservations near their old homes,
but the nations as nations were removed. The whites were
shameless. Of a quarter million dollars supposedly paid for
Creek lands, well over half were open bribes to individual
chiefs. White drums knew only one beat: move-move-
move. The deportation of the Choctaw came in 1832, the
Chickasaw in 1832–34, some of the Seminole in 1836,
the Creek in 1836–40, and the Cherokee in 1838–39.

The Indians were forced to sell their farms, equipment,
and animals at tremendous financial loss. There was little
attempt to put a good face on what amounted to armed

robbery. Indians who were considered rebellious were locked in stockades. Old friends were treated with the same abruptness as old enemies. Not even the wealthy Indians or the whites who had intermarried could get their usual special treatment. The removal was to be a removal of entire peoples with no exceptions. The journey itself was nothing less than a death march. One quarter of the Cherokee people died on what came to be called the Trail of Tears. The Indians were often chained together. They were never allowed to rest, to look after their sick, or to bury their dead. Whether or not promised supplies were delivered, the soldiers forced the Indians onward. Even the strongest were badly weakened by the long journey from the Southeast to the dusty territory called Oklahoma. Many who survived the Trail of Tears would soon die trying to live in the unfamiliar new land.

The nations facing removal sent written protests to the government. If nothing else, they hoped these official documents would establish the illegality of their removal. They thought that one day just courts would return their lands and property, a desperate hope in the American democracy which never materialized. The last Cherokee council before removal drafted a statement presenting the final word on whether or not the Indians had consented to be removed from their homeland:

> The Cherokee people have neither by themselves nor their representatives given such consent. It follows that the original title and ownership of lands still rests in the Cherokee Nation, unimpaired and absolute. The Cherokee people have existed as a distinct national community for a period extending into antiquity beyond the dates and records and memory of man. These attributes cannot be dissolved by the expulsion of the Nation from its territories by the power of the United States government.

GUERRILLAS
OF THE EVERGLADES

The Seminole in Florida were determined to die in combat before being driven out by the whites. Their territory contained a natural fortress unique among the nations—the Everglades. This vast wild area of swamps and grasses had never been completely explored. Pink flamingos, blue heron, yellow warblers, white ibis, purple gallinule, red woodpeckers, and other brilliantly colored birds circled by thousands and by the tens of thousands. Only a hurricane had the strength to beat down the thick saw-blade grass, but the Everglades always renewed itself after each storm, growing more lush and extravagant than ever. Cypress trees dominated certain sectors as alligators and turtles scavenged by the shore. Masses of water weeds and hyacinths were packed solid as if they were growing in solid earth. Beneath this web of greens and flowers laced with crawling beasts, insects, and reptiles of every description was one of the most unique rock formation in the world: hundreds of thousands of acres of fantastically shaped rock that heaved and wiggled into pinnacles, domes, pyramids, stalagmites, and subterranean caverns. Often long deep cracks split the earth as the greatest mangrove forest in the hemisphere pushed its roots deeper and deeper into the earth. The Everglades had existed with its secrets ever since the continent first hurled itself from the ocean depths. The glades seemed indestructible, yet within two hundred years the wasteful whites would chew away its edges and drain off its waters until the strange rock that seemed from another planet began to surface. The birds would die. The Indians would dwindle. Tourists would come to be thrilled by the tiny patches of what had been the ancient wilderness. But during the springtime of American power, the Everglades was as mighty as it had ever been and the Seminole were among its beloved.

The rest of Florida was as bountiful as its wild heart. The Spanish explorers had imagined that a Fountain of Youth must surely be hidden somewhere in the fertile paradise. Blooming flowers of every shape and color mingled with the different shades and textures of green in trees, shrubs, and grasses. Pumpkins, beans, and corn rose up in small clearings of fertile soil. The Seminole loved their land with the passion of a people who excel at the feast and the dance. At their Great Corn Ceremony they paid homage to the forces that had given them such a splendid country. They imitated animals and birds with special dances and songs, tossing their heads joyfully to the music of the universe. They were at one with each other and all that lived around them.

The United States was determined to control Florida. After pressuring the Spanish into selling them the peninsula, white officials gathered a group of Seminole chiefs and got them to cede most of their land in return for a reservation which the whites pledged never to invade. The whites also promised to furnish farm tools, livestock, food rations, and cash. Most of the village councils had fears about the plans but they agreed for the sake of peace. They quickly discovered the new territory to be unsuitable for their style of agriculture. Many areas even lacked drinkable water. But the Seminole were willing to rebuild their lives if they could avoid a war. They did not yet realize that the whites would never be content until they had everything and that the greediest ones already wanted the lands which still remained Seminole. The Indians did not know that the white guarantees, which were supposed to last as long as the grass shall grow and the water flow, were promises spoken upon the wind and written upon water.

The Seminole nation had been born in rebellion. *Isit,* their Creek name, meant broken off or runaway people, for the Seminole bands had broken from the Creek to create independent communities. A typical Seminole village contained some thirty family dwellings. Each unit had two structures, a two-story house for the head of the family and a one-story house for cooking and sleeping. A family garden was nearby, and farther away the tribe had a communal garden. Each family contributed to a public food supply for visitors and the village poor. The Seminole were industrious people who worked hard at planting, taking care of their animals, and trading. Their impressive dugout canoes carved from cypress trunks carried them as far as Cuba and the Bahamas. The Seminole thought of themselves as a nation but they had no central authority. A mutual respect, an informal code of behavior, and a loosely defined common religion were enough to bring communal identity to the scattered and independent villages.

Like all the tribes of the Southeast, the Seminole had blacks living with them, but the proud and rebellious Seminole treated blacks differently than most nations of the Americas did. Only some of the blacks were slaves. The others were free individuals who had run away from slavery. The Seminole gave such people sanctuary and took them as tribal members. Even slaves got good treatment. They usually lived by themselves in their own villages, ran their own affairs, and grew their own crops, only part of which had to be given to their owners. The Seminole would not sell a slave if he did not give his consent and they were reluctant to split up families. Slaves were sometimes

Osceola, the most famous of the Seminole chiefs, wrote, "You
have guns, and so have we.—You have powder and lead, and so
have we.—Your men will fight, and so will ours—until the last
drop of Seminole blood has moistened the dust of his last hunting ground." (*Courtesy of Museum of the American Indian, Heye
Foundation*)

adopted as members of a Seminole family, and the freeing
of slaves was a common practice. A slave could marry a
Seminole and their children were considered free. Mixed
bloods and blacks became chiefs and sub-chiefs in the regular Seminole settlements. Osceola, the most famous of all

the Seminole leaders, had a black sub-chief, and Coacoochee would end his career trying to form a nation of blacks
and Indians on the Rio Grande. Rather than viewing
blacks as inferiors, the Seminole admired the spirit of rebellion which had caused the blacks to seek them out.
They admired the agricultural skills the blacks had to
teach. They found their ideas about marriage and religion
were similar. Blacks had good stories to tell by the campfire
and blacks were only too happy to use Seminole drums and
rattles to show new dances and sing exciting new songs. By
the early 1800s, there were many blacks who spoke only
the Seminole languages and who lived and thought as
members of the Seminole nation.

The proslavery forces in the United States were dis-
turbed by the life blacks could find among the Seminole.
Many escaped slaves might not have revolted if they did
not have the hope of reaching Florida. The Seminole had
to be dealt with for the same reasons all Indians had to be
conquered but they must also be conquered because of
the blacks among them. As the fighting between the
United States and the Seminole began, the blacks proved to
be the angriest and most courageous warriors. They had already known one life of slavery and did not intend to return
to it. The white generals would describe them as "intrepid
hostile warriors." In truth, the most rebellious blacks and
the most rebellious Indians were united in what would be
one of the most bitter of all the Indian wars.

The first serious attempt to remove the Seminole to reservations in the West came in 1832 when the United
States convinced a few chiefs to transport their people to
Oklahoma to be "reunited" with the Creek. The village
councils, however, would have nothing to do with the plan,
and the government had to call for a second meeting. This

grand council was held in 1834, and all the respected Seminole leaders attended. The most remarkable figure was Osceola, a warrior who had come to the Seminole after his Upper Creek village was destroyed in the fighting of 1814. Osceola listened tensely as the whites demanded nothing less than that every Indian should leave Florida forever and that the immigration begin that very year. General Thompson headed the whites and suggested the groups start to prepare themselves at once. The Secretary of War in Washington had told Thompson to do everything short of war to make the Seminole leave. Had the Secretary been in the clearing and seen the angry warriors, he would hardly have been so foolish to believe anything less than a war would force them from their homeland.

Many warriors had accompanied their leaders to the important conference. All now withdrew to have a council. The ceremonial pipes were brought out. Religious men tried to communicate with the spirits. Different individuals spoke, and in their speaking together they came to an agreement. Florida was their home. The Being of Power who had made all creation had selected this part of the earth for them. If they abandoned their land, they abandoned the Being of Power and they abandoned themselves. When they returned to the whites, each head man said he would not go. Finally, Osceola stepped forward. "This land is ours. We want no agents." He withdrew his knife from his belt and stabbed the treaty. "This is the way I sign."

The army had expected some resistance and had taken the precaution of having seven hundred soldiers ready to deal with the four thousand men, women, and children of the Seminole nation. Would-be settlers came to forts ready to take free possession of Seminole lands as soon as the army removed them. Slave merchants waited patiently to claim all blacks as runaway slaves. Osceola and some of the Seminole leaders were held by Thompson after the conference, but he allowed them to return to their homes once they promised to move West.

White illusions about the quality and nature of Seminole resistance were shattered three days after Christmas 1835. General Thompson was the first to die, and the leader of the group that killed him was none other than Osceola. Thompson and another officer were assassinated as they went for a walk in the woods near Fort King. On the same day, fifty soldiers died when they were guided into an ambush by a black scout who thought more of the Seminole than he did of the army. That night Indian drums and liquor nourished the first confident dances of victory as scalps dried on a ten-foot sacrificial pole. The great war had begun.

Smashing raids followed in rapid succession. Small farms and large plantations were all the same to the Indians, who were prepared to burn everything to the ground and kill the whites who wanted to remain. The startled federal government quickly agreed to pay the people who had been burned out. Before long, more than eight hundred war refugees had to be put on the government welfare rolls. The Seminole grew so bold that they even attacked the forts. They had no unified central command or even a plan beyond the general objective of destroying everything that was connected to the whites. The Seminole no longer fought for glory and honor in the Indian tradition; they warred as a guerrilla army seeking to preserve the liberties of their nation.

That harvest season found the Seminole dancing the Great Corn Dance in the manner they always did while the whites cowered in their forts. General Scott was taken from command and the fighting was put in the hands of Major General Jesup, who had just defeated the Georgia Creek. Severe fighting continued all along the Seminole borders, but Jesup was able to arrange a meeting with some of the village heads. A few of the chiefs agreed to go West if their black tribesmen could go with them. Jesup agreed to the terms, and almost a thousand Seminole came to Fort Brooks to surrender. Jesup announced that he had ended the war, and the greedy slave dealers of Florida and Georgia immediately sent agents to recover their black "property." Jesup protested, but the civilian authorities told him he must order the Seminole to deliver up any black who had ever been a slave. The councils replied that the new condition was not acceptable and the agreement was void. Jesup was furious. He sent word that he would raid every Seminole settlement to recover whatever belonged to the whites. His threat was mortal. "I intend to hang every one of them who does not come in." Seminole who had come to bargain were captured and sent to Arkansas. New fighting broke out. The white settlers had to ask for another season of government rations.

Attack and counterattack remained the pattern throughout 1836 and most of 1837. Osceola had decided that Seminole resistance might have softened the white hearts to reason. When General Jesup guaranteed him safe conduct, Osceola came in to talk. The date for the conference was October 17, but Jesup did not intend to bargain. He had Osceola struck on the head, put in irons, and tossed into a cell. This was the first instance, but not the last, in which the white truce flag would be used by the highest army officials to "capture" leaders who could not otherwise be taken. The people of Florida were willing to back any and every means to remove the Seminole. A few individuals criticized Jesup's methods, but Osceola remained a prisoner. The Cherokee came to the Seminole to explain they had nothing to do with this treachery. They said such conduct offended them as much as it offended the Seminole. The Cherokee added that if the Seminole came West they could live on Cherokee land.

Young army officers entered the Seminole country with the idea of getting reputations as Indian fighters the way Harrison and Jackson had done. The fighting in Florida gave Colonel Zachary Taylor the beginning of a national image that would eventually take him to the presidency. One of Taylor's "victories" came at Lake Okeechobee on Christmas Day when he lost 26 men and had 112 wounded in a bloody engagement against Seminole led by Aripeka, Coacoochee, and the Prophet. Taylor managed to force the Seminole on to the beach, and when the small Seminole force left the battlefield, the reporters termed it a victory. An accompanying group of citizen volunteers moving in a separate column fared even worse and were not much written about.

Jesup himself was wounded shortly after the Lake Okeechobee fight when a group of 150 Seminole fought his force of almost two thousand men. From his hospital bed, Jesup wrote to Washington that the war could go on for years at an increasing cost in men and money. He called for another peace council, but again the politicians directed him to make no compromises. Once more, Jesup arrested the Indians who had come to bargain. Fearing this new treachery might cause the Seminole to attack the city of St. Augustine, Jesup sent all his prisoners, including Osceola, to a fort in South Carolina. Osceola made friends with some whites while he was at the fort, but he was a sick man. His health and spirit had been eaten away by imprisonment. Osceola died from malaria and was buried under a gravestone with this simple tribute: PROPHET & WARRIOR. Those who did not die at the fort were eventually shipped to Arkansas. Conditions of travel were so awful that many perished along the way or shortly after their arrival. Among the dead was King Philip, an important chief. Word of his death filtered back across the many miles to the camp of his son, Coacoochee, the Wild Cat, who was now a bitter and outraged patriot who would never again trust whites. Aripeka sent word to Jesup that he would never make a treaty with such a liar and that his people intended to fight as long as the grass should grow and the waters flow.

Aripeka's Mikasuki band soon proved their threats were real with a new set of attacks. When the whites chased after them, the Mikasuki did not stand and fight. They faded into the Everglades and waited for a new chance to strike. The war had become a grueling guerrilla struggle in the swamps. Army units had to make their way through thick black muck and saw-blade grass sharp as glass. The hot sun made their uniforms wet with sweat as insects bit their arms, legs, and faces. Suddenly Seminole would begin firing from hidden places on a nearby island or from positions protected by deep ponds. The whites fought valiantly and slowly inched their way to where the Seminole had been hidden, only to discover the expert red and black guerrillas, who preferred to lose territory rather than one of their brothers, had slipped away along a convenient lagoon or pathway. Large battles were rare. The Seminole struck swiftly, forever moving, forever sniping, forever carrying away their wounded, forever drawing soldiers deeper into the swamps, forever seeking to isolate a straggler. The army columns moved into the glades day after week after weary month, but there were no dramatic victories and no prospects of ultimate triumph. General Jesup's baton had been bent and now it was broken. On May 18, 1838, he was in Washington to explain why he had arrested Osceola after guaranteeing his safe conduct. Had the war been a success, all would have been forgiven. But Jesup had used every method he wished and the war was no nearer being over than the day General Thompson was killed. Jesup's defense of abusing the truce flag contained more truth than he intended. "If it was lawful to remove them, it was lawful to seize them." If.

The new American commander was Zachary Taylor, now a general. His proposal for ending the war was simple. No whites would be allowed to claim any black or mixed blood who was willing to move West. The news was greeted happily in some parts of the Everglades, as many of the fighters were waiting for such a compromise. They were anxious to resume normal ways of living. Deep in the glades, the attitude of the Mikasuki and others did not change. The Prophet bristled with defiance and said the spirits favored the Indian cause. He said the whites were just as weary of war as they were and no compromises were necessary. Even so, hundreds of Seminole began to surrender and whites moved back to some of their burned-out homesteads. General Taylor's peace seemed about to become permanent. Cities prospered. Scientists came to experiment on the land to see if they could make it flourish with the white man's magic. At another council at Fort King, fifty leaders were told the government would allow them to stay in Florida on a temporary basis. All might have gone well if some of the civilians of Georgia and Florida had been able to contain their fears. They had grown accustomed to government rations and did not want to rebuild, only to be burned out again. They feared the Indians might renew the war any time. Mammoth rallies were staged at which frenzied white speakers called for total removal of all the Seminole. Newspapers fed the unrest with fierce anti-Seminole editorials in every issue. The Seminole did not understand the white man's markings, but they understood the sound of his war drums. When they gathered for their Great Corn Dance in the autumn of Taylor's peace, the Prophet had fierce new words.

As would happen many times when tribes found themselves moving into the shadows of their fathers toward the place of the setting sun, the Prophet revealed that if the Seminole purified themselves they could drive out the invaders. They must rid themselves of all things connected with the whites and embrace traditional ways totally. Many of the chiefs who had not taken part in offensive warfare before were inspired by the Prophet's words and visions. They pledged that they, too, would fight. Young men drank the black drink that cleansed their bodies. The dances and music throbbed with new optimism and excitement.

The new raids were carried out with the energy of a people who wanted to reclaim their homeland forever. Those who had not been content to exist peacefully with the Seminole now recoiled before the assault of the Seminole at war. Farms and fields were put to the torch. Every traveler might be ambushed. No living thing was safe from Seminole anger. Defensive militias were organized. Bloodhounds were purchased. But whenever whites saw buzzards circling in the sky, they knew the Seminole had struck again. Taylor had failed in his peace effort and asked to be relieved of his assignment.

The new commander was Brigadier General Armistead. He had Indians brought in from the West to persuade their Florida relatives that removal was desirable, but the Indians told the truth. The West was bad. None of the promises had been kept. The weather was terrible. The climate was unhealthy. Feuding tribes had to live with or near each other. The journey west was a trail of agony and tears. The Seminole should not go.

The Prophet decreed that he never wanted to hear talk of the West again. If any new messenger was sent by the whites, he would be killed without a hearing. No insult to Indians was going to be left unavenged. No settlers would be allowed so much as a tent. General Armistead countered this militancy with 5000 soldiers and 1500 armed militia. In January, Armistead was told to use his war chest of $100,000 freely. Two months later he was given an additional million dollars to make a final solution of the Seminole question.

The greatest military success for the army in this period was the capture of the mother and daughter of Coacoochee. The tough chief came in under a flag of truce to negotiate a ransom with Colonel Worth. The famous leader arrived garbed in a theatrical costume he had found in a wagon of traveling players he and his men had fought. He thought the costume might impress the officers but he was not surprised when he was told his family would not be returned unless he promised to move West. Coacoochee agreed and said he would take along anyone who chose to go with him. Unfortunately for the cause of peace, a Major Childs "captured" an unwary Coacoochee as he was quietly returning to the fort with his personal followers. He was immediately put in chains and shipped to New Orleans. Colonel Worth had the chief returned to Florida when he found out what had happened and gave his apologies to the respected, now doubly embittered warrior. It was incidents such as these that made Coacoochee declare, "I was in hopes I should be killed in battle but a bullet never touched me."

Coacoochee staged entertainments at the fort to bring his friends and allies out of the glades. He told them that they would not drown in the unknown gulf as they feared, because he had been on the gulf and had returned. A few of his visitors agreed to join him. They felt it would be better to stay with a trusted leader even if it meant going to a new land. Many were tired of always needing their weapons wherever they went and always being alert that their fields and homes were not found by an army raiding party. Already there were almost three times as many soldiers against them as there were Seminole, counting women, babies, and the old. The warriors waited in the forts sadly. The women had long faces and did not smile. Many of the children and older people died.

Coacoochee and others had grown weary of a life of war, but in the deepest glades where the drums and fires of the Prophet were strongest, there was no toleration of weariness. Surrender was a forbidden word. Coacoochee sent a black messenger to talk, and the man's life was spared only from respect for the Wild Cat. Even so, the messenger was kept a prisoner for two years. Not even Coacoochee would be allowed to spread the poison of removal. A woman spoke of going West and was killed by her brother. Undecided tribesmen were killed. The army offered gifts and the Prophet refused them. The army sent new pledges and the Prophet refused to hear them. The army sent raiders and the warriors fought them. The army captured an occasional isolated family and the warriors tried to rescue them. The army burned down a field and the Seminole replanted. Nothing was going to convince them to change their ways or to leave the land of their fathers. The army might burn every field and village and the Seminole could still survive. The Everglades was a good mother whose deer, fish, cabbage, bananas, and other foods could sustain the Seminole forever.

The American soldiers grew tougher and smarter the longer they had to fight in the swamps. They fought in small groups like Indians. Their goals might be a single growing spot or the home of an isolated family. Days might be spent in achieving these simple objectives. Catching one warrior was an outstanding accomplishment. The war was unspectacular but as deadly as ever. A single rifle shot from a cypress or mangrove tree and a young soldier would be dead. A few aging chiefs played another game. They came to the forts to accept gifts in exchange for listening to the advantages of life in the West. They always hesitated about giving a firm reply. Always they ended by saying they must return to the council and talk it over with the young men. Sometimes the whites seized them and sometimes they let them go. The government was growing impatient over the dirty little war that would not end. Fresh units were sent into battle. Fifty-five cypress dugouts went into action. New forts arose. Finally, a simple solution to the black problem was found, a solution that might have saved thousands of lives and millions of dollars had it been adopted at the time the ultimatum for removal was presented to Osceola and the other chiefs. All blacks would go West. If a slave-owner could prove any given individual was a runaway, the government would pay the former owner the market price for such a slave.

A few bands straggled in under the new conditions, but it was too late for such compromises. The Seminole had paid too high a price to give up for so little. Scalps continued to be taken. The number of free Seminole declined as the army whittled away at the population by capturing small parties and families. The Indians struck back whenever possible and they struck with the fury of a people who had no place to retreat. Rescues of captured Seminole were frequent enough for the army to send prisoners West regularly. Coacoochee was included among the new groups to be deported. As he saw the Florida coast disappear, he spoke as so many Indians were doomed to speak, "It was my home. I loved it and to leave it now is like my burying my wife and child."

The Seminole had been weakened, but the eagle also knew exhaustion. A continuing war of attrition might eventually have accomplished genocide or total removal, but the Seminole had made the cost too high. Colonel Worth called for a council to be held in August of 1842 to make a peace. The Seminole were to be allowed to remain in Florida and their reservation would be within the part of the Everglades they now held as well as in a neutral zone in which neither whites nor Indians could settle.

Colonel Worth thought all the head men would respond, but the record of treachery, broken promises, and bitter warfare was not so easily overcome. Aripeka said he liked the terms but he was too old to sign anything. The Prophet said the terms were acceptable but that he had lost his power and could not sign. Octiarche, the

In 1908 Seminole children like these were still growing up in the Everglades. (*Courtesy of Museum of the American Indian, Heye Foundation*)

brother of Coacoochee, said he would have nothing to do with white men. Only old Billy Bowlegs and a few aged warriors attended the conference. Bowlegs agreed to be responsible for the conduct of the Seminole as long as the whites behaved themselves. Four moons later all military units except for one regiment were withdrawn. A year later Worth was made a general and given a new post. There would be Seminole outbreaks again but never a full scale war like those now ended.

Eight bloody summers had passed since Osceola had plunged his knife into the white demands. A nation of four thousand had fought a nation of millions. More than three thousand whites had perished in a struggle a few overconfident leaders had thought seven hundred blue-coats could prevent. Forty to sixty million dollars had been spent to equip armies, pension settlers, and re-build destroyed property. Millions of acres had gone un-planted year after year. When the histories of the period were written, the war would be termed a Seminole de-feat, but in the end, at least three hundred Seminole re-mained to live as they had chosen to live. They never surrendered and they never signed a single treaty. They had left such a legacy of heroism and pride that even in the twentieth century many of their descendants would refuse to learn the white man's tongue. Their defiance was an echo of some of the last words of Osceola, "They could not capture me except under a white flag. They cannot hold me except with a chain."

IN THE LAND BEYOND
THE FATHER OF WATERS

The Seminole who survived the transplanting to the West were placed near the other tribes of the old Southeast. Not all the promises about the West were broken, but prosperity came only to those individuals who ceased to behave in the ways of the past. In the Everglades, people were judged according to ability. A healer, whether male or female, must heal or be replaced. A leader must show wisdom or be removed from office. In the new place, the measure of recognition was wealth. Rich tribal members owned the best lands and schemed to increase their holdings, while the poor were shoved into the back country and forced to sell their labor. The rich came to own many slaves and took up commercial farming methods.

The Seminole were the most hesitant of the five nations about accepting the new ways, and Coacoochee was one of the least yielding. The tough chief was concerned that his black families might be kidnaped by slavers and that all his people might come under the power of unfriendly tribes. Most of all, he found it intolerable to live under regulations set by strangers and enemies. He got permission to make trips to Washington, D.C., and to the Everglades and to other Indian nations seeking allies in a scheme to form a new Indian and black nation in an area of the Rio Grande controlled by Mexico. His plans never materialized on the scale he sought, but he eventually moved to the Rio Grande with forty warriors and their families. In time over five hundred blacks came to live in his territory. Coacoochee's life and dreams were cut short in 1857 when he died from smallpox. His life had been a constant struggle to survive, yet in his final years the Wild Cat at last fulfilled his Seminole heritage by coming to live on his own terms. Unlike so many of his tragedy-stricken people, Coacoochee was able to die in the freedom he had been born to.

The Seminole who remained on the reservations came together with the other Southeast tribes in 1859 to form the Federation of the Five Civilized Nations. Less than two years later, the outbreak of the American Civil War brought disaster. Most of the influential leaders owned slaves, and the councils voted to support the Confederacy. Union sympathizers were driven from the villages and many of them suffered from hunger and other hardships. A Cherokee general was the last major Confederate officer

Seminole warriors continued to move quietly through the swamps in 1910, more than seventy years after their long war with the United States, and to this day they can be found in the land of their ancestors. (*Courtesy of Museum of the American Indian, Heye Foundation*)

to surrender, but when the Union armies finished their pillage of Indian territory, there was little consolation in an honor based on gutted homes and ravaged plantations. The Indians had once again made the fundamental error of taking part in a war between the whites in the mistaken belief they would be treated as equals. The very Washington politicians who undertook the most lenient policy possible in relation to white southern rebels treated the Indians with vengeance. They declared that by taking part in the rebellion the Indians had broken their treaties. They must now give up the best parts of Oklahoma as a punishment. They must give up other parts of their reservations so that newly removed tribes could have a place to live. They must allow the railroad free passage. The demands went on paragraph after paragraph. Whatever the whites desired, the Indians must give. Even on the rare occasion when a new law was meant to be beneficial, shrewd lawyers and businessmen saw that the Indians were cheated. Most laws showed no respect for tribal customs and communal values. The attempt of the Indians to preserve their identity by entering the Union as the state of Sequoya in 1905 was denied. The admission of the same territory in 1907 under the name of Oklahoma was accompanied by the official dissolving of tribal governmental authority. Most Indians were soon reduced to poverty, although some individuals became important persons and were even elected to the highest state offices. The price for such individual success was the abandonment of what was distinctly Indian. The red nation was not invited to make its contribution to the American melting pot but to dissolve without a trace.

Indian ways survived only in the Seminole remnant left in the Everglades. The Seminole found more and more remote areas of the swamps to live in. They resisted all efforts to change their ways of living. The occasional armed conflicts were troublesome but the Everglades was a loving fortress and a few hidden fields provided enough food for survival. Life could be precarious some years but each harvest the Seminole were able to dance the Great Corn Dance as their ancestors had. They were able to preserve that elemental humanism which had made it so easy for them to accept runaway blacks as equals and so impossible for them to trade their new black brothers and sisters for political advantage. The United States grew to be the most powerful nation mankind had ever known, but the Seminole who remained in the Everglades were unrelenting spiritual enemies. Even as you read these words, the Seminole are still walking in the swamps their ancestors would not forsake. They remain the unconquered.

Sitting Bull, more a spiritual leader than a war chief, posed for this photograph which became extremely popular with "the folks back East." (*Courtesy of Museum of the American Indian, Heye Foundation*)

PART III

The Sacred Hoop: The Great Plains

A few more passing suns will see us here no more, and our dust will mingle with these same prairies. I see as in a vision the dying spark of our council fires, the ashes cold and white. I see no longer the curling smoke rising from our lodge poles. I hear no longer the songs of the women as they prepare the meal. The antelope have gone; the buffalo wallows are empty. Only the wail of the coyote is heard. The white man's medicine is stronger than ours; his iron horse rushes over the buffalo trail. He talks to us through his whispering wire. We are like birds with broken wings. My heart is cold within me. My eyes are growing dim—I am old.

Chief Plenty Coups (Crow)

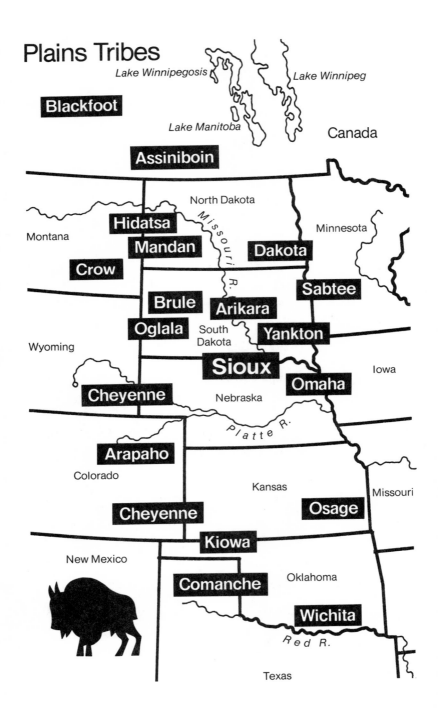

Plains Tribes

Lake Winnipegosis

Lake Winnipeg

Blackfoot

Lake Manitoba

Canada

Assiniboin

North Dakota

Missouri R.

Montana

Hidatsa

Mandan

Minnesota

Dakota

Crow

Sabtee

Brule

Arikara

Oglala

South
Dakota

Yankton

Wyoming

Sioux

Iowa

Omaha

Cheyenne

Nebraska

Platte R.

Arapaho

Colorado

Kansas

Missouri

Cheyenne

Osage

Kiowa

New Mexico

Comanche

Oklahoma

Wichita

Red R.

Texas

THE SEVEN COUNCIL FIRES
OF THE SIOUX

Between the Father of Waters and the Rocky Mountains, fifty million buffalo grazed upon grasses that had never known the press of a wheel. A big herd blackened the earth for miles and took days to cross large rivers. The proud horsemen who hunted them regarded the buffalo as gifts from the spirits. On the eastern plains the tribes were called Assiniboin, Mandan, Hidatsa, Arikara, Omaha, and Osage. In the south they were Cheyenne, Kiowa, Wichita, Comanche, and Caddo. By the great plateaus of the west, Blackfoot, Crow, and Bannock. The most famous of them among the whites were the seven tribes known collectively as the Sioux. Army officers grudgingly termed them good shots, good riders, the best fighters the sun ever shone on. No group of Indians fought more bravely for their ways or mourned more profoundly at their loss than these regal buffalo hunters.

The Sioux were a tall and slender people proud of their long black hair and their reddish brown skin. Their facial features varied from looking like northern or southern Europeans to resembling the Asian people. Buffalo Bill Cody, the enterprising scout and showman, featured Sioux in his spectacular Wild West Show so often that their stunning feather bonnets and their pleasant speech of soft consonants became the prototype for all Indians in the minds of most of the world, an image reinforced in the twentieth century by Hollywood movies.

The Sioux were divided into three major subdivisions, the Eastern or Santee Sioux made up of four tribes, the Yankton Sioux made up of two tribes, and the Teton Sioux who outnumbered the other six tribes combined. The seven fires of the council were almost never lit at the same time and place for a common purpose and at no time did all seven tribes wage war against their enemies simultaneously. The Sioux Council was an invention that served as a cultural unifier rather than as a political mechanism. The Sioux called themselves the Dakota, a word meaning *friend* or *ally*.

There was far more contact among subdivisions within one of the seven tribes than among the separate groups. The Teton Sioux became the most famous among whites and Indians alike, and the greatest Teton war chiefs came from the Oglala subtribe, which produced men such as Red Cloud and Crazy Horse. Other Teton subtribes were the Brulé, the Miniconjou, the Sans Arcs, the Two Kettles, the Blackfoot Sioux, and Sitting Bull's people, the Hunkpapa.

The lives of the Sioux were the most poetic of all the tribes and became an important part of the legend of the West. The Sioux were often called the vision seekers because their main religious activity was to seek visions or dreams, which they believed were sent to them by the spirits. Young men would camp in cold and terrifying places in order to induce dreams. A vision which occurred during the teen years might provide the material for a lifetime of meditation. More important than personal visions were visions dealing with the problems of the nation. Each of the Sioux tribes gathered once a year to seek communal visions in a ceremony called the Sun

Dance. This was the one event that brought together the separate groups of this warrior-dominated society.

The Sun Dance procedures lasted for almost two weeks. The various subtribes camped in an immense circle, the ancient symbol of unbreakable unity. Specific individuals hoped to receive messages from the supernaturals through a ritual involving self-inflicted pain. One of the first steps was for the men to construct an immense red tepee in the center of the camp. It was here that the vision seekers would smoke, fast, pray, and prepare various ceremonial objects. The women had a sacred gathering of their own at which a virgin was chosen to strike down the tree to be used as the main pole for the Sun Dance itself. As the feast progressed, mock battles were staged between the various soldier societies. Every age level and each sex found some step or song to contribute to the unity of the tribe. Everything led up to the seeking of visions, which occurred in the last three days when the purified ones came forward and had sharp skewers placed under their breast muscles. The skewers were fastened to the Sun Dance pole some twenty to thirty feet away by thongs. The dancer had to try to tear himself free while the rest of the gathering sang, prayed, and pitied him. If he fainted from pain and exhaustion before getting free, he could have someone pull the skewers loose. A man who could actually wrench himself free was considered to have powerful "medicine." Sitting Bull danced the Sun Dance just before the Custer fight and he dreamed that "soldiers fell into my camp." Throughout his long career, Sitting Bull had considerable political influence, for the Sioux held that spiritual power was a crucial element in all decision making.

The Sioux said, "It is better to die a young man on the

battlefield than to live to carry a cane," but such sayings
were believed to be true in a poetic rather than a factual
sense. The death of a young warrior was always considered
a great tragedy demanding the most sacred rituals. The
Sioux fought often but they fought mainly for glory. In
one ten-year war between the Ojibway and the Sioux, only
two hundred persons died in populations numbering over
ten thousand. Victory or defeat or stalemate were all regarded as equally valid endings to any particular combat.
The important thing was that fighting had taken place. A
few scalps sufficed to make a success and many war parties
came home with no scalps at all. A man who could touch a
living enemy still protected by his fighting comrades was
considered to have achieved the ultimate in bravery. Such
a feat was called counting coup.

Coups of various degrees were awarded in an elaborate
scoring system for the Sioux regarded war as a sport or
game, an activity for leisure time. Men often rode into
battle with coup sticks, which were not weapons at all but
ordinary sticks adorned with medicine symbols. A minor
coup was scored by being the first to touch the body of a
man just killed. All coups had to be witnessed by other
warriors so that later the man who had counted coup
could safely boast of his exploit at the campfire and paint
pictures of his deeds on the outside of his tepee. The
warrior societies often had to sit in council to judge if a
given act was worthy of a coup feather and if so, of what
degree. The eagle feather was notched or tasseled to show
the importance of the coup. The angle at which the feather
was worn was another indication of importance. A single
eagle feather worn straight up in the hair was far more
prestigious than a colorful bonnet which only had decora-
tive value.

Most of the Sioux warriors did not enjoy fighting the soldiers of the United States because warfare with the bluecoats was boring. Even when it came to serious political questions, the Sioux held it elemental that it was best to live a long time and fight many battles rather than to perish in a foolish act. One who gave away his life cheaply was to be pitied rather than honored. Not even a war chief had unquestionable authority. He could say, "Follow me," and if enough men followed, he had a fighting force. Such haphazard discipline saved the Sioux from such slaughters as the white soldiers were periodically caught in, but the same lack of discipline meant they usually lost opportunities to crush their enemies after having stunned them with an initially successful attack. When a Sioux war party found their enemies had prepared good defenses, they considered it common sense to ride away without a fight. Fighting was as natural and pleasant to them as eating although on rare occasion they could become involved in vengeful feuds. Generally war was something to do after the last buffalo hunt in the period before the coming of the snows. As with the Cherokee, it was a beloved occupation.

Sioux military skills represented only one of the four basic male virtues, which were bravery, fortitude, generosity, and wisdom. An oracle such as Sitting Bull might excel in wisdom and a war chief such as Crazy Horse in bravery, but every man was expected to embody each of the virtues as much as possible. Sioux ideals were very concrete ways of behaving and judging. Had the war chief lost many men in his last raid? How many horses had he captured? How many times he had counted coup? Had a man possessed the fortitude to dance the Sun Dance? Had he gone to a frightening place to seek a vision? Did the man who claimed to be generous give away many gifts? Were the orphans, lamed, and old in his village cared for? How had he divided the food during the blizzard?

The four female virtues of bravery, fortitude, truthfulness, and childbearing could have been just as rigorous, but they were only a cover for the inferior social status of all women. Only truthfulness and childbearing were stressed. These were the virtues which defined a woman's reputation through her relationship to her man. Even a woman who was a dreamer or a healer could increase her stature by being a mother. The virtue of truthfulness was mainly a device to test a woman's sexual fidelity and to prevent campfire gossip. Virginity before marriage and loyalty afterwards were the ideals presented to women even though a man could do anything he wished. Men were even allowed to disfigure disloyal wives, and divorce for a man was a simple matter of sounding a drum and saying, "Whoever wants her can have her. Come get her. I do not want her any more." Men with more than one wife were common, and the second wife was usually a younger sister of the first. A few men took as many as six wives, but general Sioux opinion was that two were more than enough for one man. Women did all the menial work, but the men were obliged to hunt and raid for all the people they had taken responsibility for.

Unmarried Sioux women perfected their quilting and embroidery skills to show what good wives they would make. They left work such as tanning hides to older women because such tasks made hands rough. The official manner of courting these young women was for the suitor to stand by her tepee. If she chose to come out, he would wrap his blanket around them and they would stand and talk. The informal methods were far more exciting and showed the good humor of most of Sioux life. Young men with love potions hidden on their bodies lingered about the lodges of maidens. Certain tunes played on a big twisted cedar flute were considered irresistible if played in the right surroundings. Thus, would-be lovers waited with their flutes for maidens sent to do a chore, and anxious parents had to provide chaperones whenever an eligible daughter left their sight. The flutes and potions were everywhere and the maidens were not unwilling. Parents sometimes bound the feet of their daughters at night, but their main concern was for a good marriage, not punishment. The genuine love and concern Sioux felt for each other made up for some of the harsher aspects of their male-dominated sex codes.

Much of a man's life was concerned with the activities of his society or fraternity. These groups included distinguished warriors, former shamans, retired hunters, and honored head men. They gave opinions on weighty matters and saw that the rituals were correctly carried out. The society usually organized all hunting and war parties. One of their most important duties came if they were selected to be police of a hunt. The society was then expected to see that all hunting rules were observed and that the tribe hunted as a unit rather than individually. The police decided which hunters were to receive various cuts of the slain beasts. Any tribesman who broke the rules of the hunt or other codes of the tribe was first reprimanded in his society and given a chance to reform. Only if he persisted in his mistakes would he be taken before the tribal council. The worst punishment for an Indian who would not abide by tribal customs was banishment. To be alone was considered a far harsher judgment than to die.

The buffalo was critical to every Sioux need. The typical Sioux tepee consisted of some twenty buffalo hides sewn into a great tent braced by ten to twenty poles interlocked at the top. Rather than crude affairs, these tepees were extremely graceful and strong enough to withstand powerful winds. The tepees were often decorated with colorful geometric patterns or painted with pictures showing important coups. Tepee furniture consisted of couches, beds, and blankets made of buffalo hide. For the difficult winter months there were impressive buffalo robes trimmed with ermine and feathers. Buffalo meat was the tribe's main food; buffalo muscles provided bowstrings, and buffalo bones, knives. Many tribes believed all the continent and the Unseen as well was ruled by a Great Buffalo, who pitied man and beast alike. Both their religion and their practical needs caused the Sioux to be thoughtful conservationists. Often, they apologized to Great Buffalo for their need to slay other animals.

Horses had been native to North America during prehistoric times but the animal had died out and was unknown to the Indians until they saw the Europeans riding them. The tribes of the eastern woodlands found the new animal convenient, but they did not change their basic way of living. The Apache, the tough thin fists of the deserts, had little use for them, eating the creature as often as riding it. On the Great Plains, however, the horse brought new prosperity. Formerly men had to stalk the buffalo on foot, a time consuming, tricky, and tiresome method of hunting. Various crops had to be planted around the permanent camps in case the hunt was unsuccessful or the herds left their summer feeding grounds early. Dogs were needed to carry heavy loads and traveling was slow and unpleasant.

Before the coming of the whites, fifty million buffalo roamed the Great Plains between the Mississippi River and the Rocky Mountains. (*Courtesy of Museum of the American Indian, Heye Foundation*)

Horses changed everything. Hunters could streak after buffalo on horseback and be sure of a kill almost every time. Instead of waiting for buffalo to come to them, hunting parties could ride out to wherever they might be grazing. There was no longer any danger of there not being enough meat so the Sioux could give up almost all farming. With hunting and traveling so much easier, and planting almost eliminated, there was much more leisure time to paint and sing and court and fight. The Sioux enjoyed life as never before.

Until the 1840s, Sioux contacts with the whites were slight. Some tribesmen had traveled to the Southwest where they had bought or stolen horses, but in general they only knew about the whites from stories told by other tribes. Early in the century, Lewis and Clark passed through their lands on their monumental exploration of the Louisiana Purchase. Later, Tecumseh pleaded with the eastern groups to join his confederation. A few bands fought for the British occasionally, but after the War of 1812, the eastern tribes became disgusted with the red-coats. One chief told them exactly what he thought of their honor:

> After we have fought for you, endured many hardships, lost some of our people and awakened the vengeance of our power-ful neighbors, you make a peace for yourselves and leave us to obtain such terms as we can! You no longer need our service, and offer us these goods to pay us for having deserted us. But no, we will not take them. We hold them and yourselves in equal contempt!

The earliest trappers who came to the Sioux were more like white brothers than enemies. They brought guns and other equipment which they gladly traded for hides. They were few and many took Sioux wives and lived as the Indian lived. The Sioux treated them with the hospitality and generosity which was their law. Yet each year there were more whites. Apparently they were not so small a tribe as the councils had first thought. They came now in wagons and they began to frighten the buffalo. Some went down the Santa Fe Trail leading south to New Mexico and others went north to Oregon. Gold was discovered in California and more whites rushed through Sioux territories. An epidemic of cholera followed in the wake of the whites making many tribes extinct. Disputes arose and there were minor fights but the tribes were proud to fly the colorful American flag. In 1851 the eastern Sioux even gave up their land in Minnesota to show the whites they were willing to share their land.

The Sioux were not the only plains nations having conflicts with the whites and not every pressure came from the East. To the west of the Sioux lived the Cheyenne people, tribes having a life pattern similar to the Sioux and often fighting at their side as allies. In November of 1864, a group of some eight hundred Cheyenne under the leadership of Black Kettle received permission from the United States to camp near a fort in Colorado. Other groups had raided in the area for years and white civilians calling themselves the Colorado Volunteers decided that they would seek out and destroy any Indians who might make war in the future. The leader of the Volunteers was a Colonel Chivington, an itinerant preacher who hated all Indians. The Volunteers wanted more war rather than the peace agreed to by Black Kettle. They marched for two days through deep snow to come upon the Cheyenne camp with rifles and cannons blazing. Chief Black Kettle thought the surprise attack must be a mistake. He valiantly walked from his tepee carrying the American flag that had been given to him at a council in 1860. Beneath the stars and stripes he had fastened a white flag. But the Volunteers had come to kill, not to talk. They ignored both flags and within an hour had slain some five hundred Cheyenne, two thirds of them women and children. While Black Kettle and other survivors were still fleeing northward, one hundred scalps were taken to Denver where they were exhibited to wild applause and cheering between the acts of a theatrical performance. The Massacre of Sand Creek was a nightmare no Indian would ever forget or forgive.

THE WAR CHIEFS

Each year the number of wagons increased and each year
more Indians began to resist. In June of 1866 the army
came to terms with a group of head men representing two
thousand Sioux, but other bands totaling twice that number were not reconciled. The respected Red Cloud, who
had counted eighty coups, spoke for the disenchanted:

> Hear ye, Dakota! When the Great Father at Washington sent
> his chief soldier to ask for a path through our hunting grounds,
> a way for his iron road to the mountains and the western sea, we
> were told that they wished merely to pass through our country,
> not to tarry among us, but to seek for gold in the far west. Our
> old chiefs thought to show their friendship and good will, when
> they allowed this dangerous snake in our midst . . . Yet before
> the ashes of the council fires are cold, the Great Father is
> building his forts among us. You have heard the sound of the
> white soldier's axe upon the Little Piney. His presence here is
> an insult and a threat. It is an insult to the spirits of our an-
> cestors. Are we to give up their sacred graves to be plowed for
> corn? Dakotas, I am for war!

The advance Red Cloud sought to rally his people
against was the opening of the Bozeman Trail which was
to be a short cut through Sioux Country to the new
mines in Montana. Three forts and several stations made
up the life line of the new trail. One of the most important parts of the complex was Fort Kearny built on the
banks of the Little Piney River, and it was against Fort
Kearny that Red Cloud began his war. During the last
five months of 1866, there were fifty-one separate attacks
on Kearny, but the effort was not a formal siege. The
garrison was never isolated by a closed ring of enemies,

The first of the four leaders of this group of Crow warriors carrying coup sticks is Plenty Coups who said, "We are like birds with broken wings." (*Courtesy of Museum of the American Indian, Heye Foundation*)

and a wood gathering detachment went out every day. Supplies arrived more or less regularly. Even the mail came through. But the Sioux were always there and threatening. On December 21 word reached the fort that the wood train was again under attack. Brevet Lieutenant Colonel William Fetterman asked to lead a party of eighty-one to the rescue. He boasted, "Give me eighty men and I'll ride through the whole Sioux nation." His commanding officer told him to be wary of ambush but Fetterman chased after the first decoy party he saw and his entire command was wiped out.

The Sioux didn't follow up their slaughter of Fetterman in any specific way but simply continued their previous tactics. A month later the army took revenge at the Wagon

Box Fight. A party of from two to three thousand Sioux had attacked a column of troops on wood detail and in one part of the battle some five hundred braves had isolated three dozen soldiers near their wagons. The Indians lined up confident that their enemies would soon join the foolish Fetterman. They charged on horseback only to discover the troops were armed with a new Springfield repeating rifle rather than the old muzzle loaders. The wall of fire did not stop after the first round and the horsemen retreated with heavy losses. Some officers, with their usual desire to impress superiors, claimed four hundred Sioux were killed, but the commander of the escort reckoned that forty Indians had been slain, a much more believable figure. The Sioux rallied after their surprise and attacked with renewed vigor but on foot and with extreme caution. The soldiers might yet have perished if a relief column armed with a howitzer cannon had not arrived from the fort to rescue them.

Ninety-two miles farther up the Bozeman Trail stood Fort Smith. No party entered or left it from November 30, 1866, through June 8, 1867. The harassed soldiers were greatly relieved when they got some of the new Springfields. During a battle called the Hayfield Fight, the Sioux again suffered heavy losses when they came up against the new rifles for the first time. But if the Sioux could not take the forts, the army was not able to operate between them. The Bozeman Trail was a failure. White officers insisted that they had not lost the war. They only needed more men and more time and more weapons and they would rid the area of the Sioux menace. Leaders in Washington thought differently and in 1868, Red Cloud was approached to discuss peace terms.

Red Cloud had lost many warriors and he understood

the ultimate problems the new rifles posed. For their part, the whites were willing to close the Bozeman Trail as the new railroads were making other routes to Montana more profitable. General Ulysses S. Grant wanted an end to the whole humiliating and costly affair. After a summer of bickering, Red Cloud agreed to a Sioux reservation that included all of what would become South Dakota west of the Missouri River. The Bozeman Trail was to be abandoned and the Sioux were allowed to burn the hated forts to the ground. The Sioux had won their first and last war with the United States.

The army reorganized itself following the end of the Civil War in 1865. Forty-six regiments of ten companies each were created. Thirty-eight of the regiments were made up of white troops, four regiments were made up of black troops, and four regiments called Veterans Reserve Corps were made up of wounded men. The army maintained the forty-six regiment size throughout the Indian wars up to the American entry into World War I. Sections of the new army soon went into action against the Sioux, Arapaho, Apache, Cheyenne, Comanche, and Kiowa. The new commander of the western armies was General Sheridan, the Union cavalry hero of the Civil War.

The army felt hostile to all the Indians but they were most upset with the Sioux, the one nation that had gained a victory over them. General Sheridan suggested in an echo of what the British General Amherst had said a hundred years before that if necessary the Sioux must be exterminated. His predecessor had made it a policy to tolerate no "insolence" from any Indian. General Sherman, using the same bloody finger he had used in marching through Georgia wrote that all Indians must go on reservations at

General Sherman and the Indian commissioners met with the Sioux in 1868 at Fort Laramie in Wyoming to discuss a treaty. (*Courtesy of Museum of the American Indian, Heye Foundation*)

once or be killed off. The generals were repeating in somewhat more sophisticated language what the saloon toughs banged with their fists—the only good Indian is a dead Indian.

The problem of dealing honorably with Indians was further complicated by the strivers who thought to use military feats as a path to political and financial power. George Armstrong Custer, who was to achieve fame in a manner he didn't quite anticipate, was just such a striver. Although he had graduated at the bottom of his West Point class and later had been court-martialed for failure to follow orders, there was no denying his physical courage. His commanding officers wrote very negatively of his personal and professional qualities, calling him untruthful and unprincipled, but his flamboyant style was attractive to Washington politicians. The common soldiers under his command distrusted him and considered his judgments reckless, but the press portrayed him as a popular leader. His strong personality and political ambition brought him influence far beyond his meager accomplishments as a warrior.

The chiefs who refused to live on reservations had no special complaints. They simply wanted to live as they had always lived, hunting buffalo and counting coup as frequently as possible. They believed that they possessed but did not own the land which they called their mother. One of their medicine men said, "Only crazy or very foolish men would sell their mother." The war leader Crazy Horse was more practical. "One does not sell the earth upon which the people walk." Sitting Bull would tell General Miles, "God made me an Indian but not an agency Indian." When Crazy Horse was invited to join Red Cloud and Spotted Tail for a tour of the East where he might shake the hand of the Great White Father in Washington, he replied, "My father is with me and there is no father between me and the Great Spirit." Gall, Two Moon, Hump, Crow King, and the other rebels believed that the only life worth having was that of being a free rider upon the prairies. Cities were for the crazy white Americans. Farming was dull and offended their religious feelings. They agreed with the Nez Percé: "The earth is my mother. Do you give me an iron plow to wound my mother's breasts? Shall I take a scythe and cut my mother's hair?"

By the seventies the Sioux way of life was under severe pressures. The buffalo slaughter was in high gear. Some of the killing was for the value of the meat, but most was a sport or a luxury industry quietly encouraged by the army,

which understood that killing the buffalo was another way
of killing Indians. Often the two-thousand-pound corpse
was left to rot, once its tongue had been cut away. In 1871
a new tanning process made it profitable to turn buffalo
hide into leather. From then on, there was no halting the
massacre. The buffalo's own stupidity made the hunting
easy. Even if one member of a herd was shot, the others
did not necessarily stampede. A clever hunter only had to
keep killing any animal that seemed about to run. A hundred buffalo might be killed in one spot, and a hunter
could kill thousands in a month. Lazy hunters sometimes
simply stampeded the animals until they fell over cliffs.
The ponderous buffalo had been able to withstand the
needs of a hundred tribes and the fury of thousands of
blizzards, but the white man's dollar economy proved to
be a fatal foe.

Black Elk of the Oglala was bewildered. "The white men
did not kill them to eat; they killed them for the metal that
makes them crazy, and they only took the hides to sell.
Sometimes they did not take the hides, only the tongues;
and I have heard that fireboats came down the Missouri
with dried bison tongues. You can see that they who did
this were crazy." By 1880 the slaughter of the northern
herds was complete. The Indians rode as far as the western
mountains but there were no more herds to hunt, no hides
or meat to see them through that winter or any winter
thereafter. Only skulls, bones, and horns remained, and
these were gathered by the children of settlers to be sold as
souvenirs to tourists passing through on trains.

The Indians did not perceive how total the end of their
life style would be but they knew that the whites thought
in a different way than they did. The Sioux considered everything that lived as something sacred. Black Elk ex-

pressed their creed unforgettably, "Is not the sky a father and the earth a mother and are not all living things with feet and wings and roots their children?" Later the remarkable medicine man would travel in Buffalo Bill's circus to the lighted cities of the East and to the capitals of Europe, where his eyes would even gaze upon the Queen of England. Black Elk sought some secret that would save his people, but his conclusions were as somber as they were realistic,

> I did not see anything to help my people. I could see that the white people did not care for each other the way our people did before the nation's hoop was broken. They would take everything from each other if they could, and so there are some who had more of everything than they could use, while crowds of people had nothing at all, and maybe were starving. They had forgotten that the earth was their mother.

Crazy Horse and the other war chiefs were not always able to express themselves so brilliantly, but they understood that civilizations were in collision, that something more significant than tribal markings and technological devices separated them. The Sioux warriors vowed they would fight until the evergreens should all turn yellow.

The Black Hills in South Dakota had been promised to the Indians for as long as the grass shall grow and the waters flow. The Black Hills were more than a pleasant hunting ground. They were considered sacred territory charged with particular spiritual significance for the seven nations of the council fires, a place where supernaturals dwelled, a holy place. The small mountains stood out dramatically from the surrounding plain. Ponderosa pine, chilly streams, striking rock formations, and lovely canyons made it an ideal place for thinking and dreaming. The Indians loved the Black Hills because they were a place of beauty; the whites coveted them because they believed the Black Hills contained "the metal that makes them crazy."

Custer led a group of soldiers on to the sacred grounds in 1874. Although the official explanation for the move was that Custer was to clear the region of any non-Sioux Indians and to drive away all settlers who were violating the treaty, Custer's real mission was to survey the area for a fort and for a possible railroad route, a clear indication the army intended to see the Sioux removed from their sacred grounds. Custer conveniently included geologists in his party to investigate the possibility that the Black Hills contained gold. Newsmen also happened to be invited and they obliged by giving wide and exaggerated publicity to the positive findings of the scientists. Custer was so brazen he even brought along miners. The Sioux were soon calling Custer "Chief of all the Thieves." The federal government offered to buy the land from the Sioux but Spotted Tail and Red Cloud named a price they knew the United States would never agree to. Some prospectors tried to purchase mining rights but most just moved in, confident the army would not attempt to dislodge them. The army sent a few patrols into the hills but the number of miners multiplied until the Sioux began to burn wagons and take scalps on their own. By 1875 the Gold Rush was in full swing and the United States Government had decided to crack down on all Indians who had not agreed to treaties. An order went out in early December that any Indian who did not report to a reservation in two months would be dealt with by the military. The insincerity of the government was obvious. No Indian in his right mind would travel the bitter winter trails for the privilege of becoming a prisoner.

The Non-Treaties spent most of their time in Wyoming. They fought the Crow constantly and occasionally they raided the few white settlers in the area. Their exact numbers are difficult to determine. They were at least five thousand and most likely as numerous as ten thousand. In the springtime two to four thousand of the Agency or Treaty Sioux would join them for the hunting. The army imagined it could handle the Non-Treaties quickly and remove the shame of having lost Red Cloud's War. The military did not know it was riding to even greater humiliations than the closing of the Bozeman Trail and to greater dishonor than Sand Creek.

General Crook led a force of 1325 soldiers accompanied by Crow scouts in an effort to locate the lodges of the hostiles. On the morning of June 17 near the banks of the Rosebud, 1500 Sioux and Cheyenne met him to defend their camps. The Indian commander was Crazy Horse, whose successful raiding had already raised him to legendary status. Probably the most skillful war leader the Sioux ever produced, Crazy Horse is said to have led the attack with the cry, "Hoka hey! Follow me! Today is a good day to fight! Today is a good day to die!" His forces swept forward in a dazzling sequence of hit and run attacks that spread Crook's troops along a wide front. Crook tried to relieve the pressure by sending a force into the valley of Rosebud Creek to destroy some Sioux villages, but he had to recall them as the men of Crazy Horse threatened to break his lines. This was not the small guerrilla raid of traditional Plains warfare but a formal military battle. The new Indian determination impressed Crook, and he recorded that the Rosebud action was among the fiercest in his long military career.

Unfortunately for the Sioux, the tribes had already lost too many wars, and even under so gifted a chief as Crazy Horse the braves would not fight in the orderly manner of

George Armstrong Custer, the ambitious Indian fighter, and Buffalo Bill Cody, the Indians' sometime friend, strike poses in keeping with their reputations as tamers of the "Wild West." (*Courtesy of Museum of the American Indian, Heye Foundation*)

the whites. Warriors still tended to take spectacular individual actions instead of concentrating their firepower in units. They still tended to leave the battlefield as soon as they made a good coup or captured a weapon. The fighting consumed a whole day with much movement on both sides and the outcome was a severe defeat for General Crook. His troops had superior weapons, including repeating rifles, but they had suffered so much from wounds, fatigue,

brush fires, and lost supplies that they were immobilized for a month. The general never saw the camps he had come to destroy. Rather than persuading hostiles to come into the reservations, he had strengthened their spirit of resistance. His larger strategy for a three-pronged attack was completely ruined. It is possible that the Indians might have won an ever greater victory had they continued the fight against the weary soldiers, but such was not their way. When the sun began to set, they broke off contact with their foes to return home to eat and celebrate. In the days which followed, rather than renew the battle, they rode off

to join the Sun Dance camp forming on the Little Bighorn River where they boasted of their triumph. They held
up captured weapons, distributed captured supplies, told
of their individual coups, and spread the word that the respected General Crook would be out of action for the rest
of the summer.

The Indians who assembled on the Little Bighorn River
made up the largest group to ever council on the Great
Plains. The dreams of Hiawatha and Tecumseh lived once
more. Large pony herds ate all the grass for miles around
and scared away the game, but the tribal circles gave the
Indians a feeling of power they had never experienced before and would never experience again. The good news of
Crazy Horse was a favorable omen from the spirits. Warriors recounted the triumphs of Red Cloud's War. Never
again would so many Indians be so certain of their
strength. Here were perhaps fifteen hundred lodges with
over five thousand warriors. The northern circles belonged
to the Cheyenne who had recently fought against the bluecoats. At the other end were the Hunkpapa of Sitting Bull,
Crow King, and Gall. Between them were the camp circles
of the Miniconjou under Hump, Sans Arc under Striped
Eagle, and Oglala under Crazy Horse, Low Dog, and Big
Road. Smaller circles were made up of Blackfoot Sioux,
Two Kettles, Yankton, Santee, and Arapaho. To complete
the elation of the congress, Sitting Bull had a vision. He
had long been renowned for his ability to control the
weather. Now, he had had fifty pieces of flesh cut from all
parts of his body as he danced the Sun Dance and the spirits had revealed that the Indians would soon have a mighty
victory.

The circular patterns of the Little Bighorn camp were
not accidental. They reflected a mystical belief about the

power of the circle based on continued observations of nature. Black Elk explained:

> You have noticed that everything an Indian does is in a circle and that is because the Power of the World always works in circles and everything tries to be round. In old days when we were a strong and happy people, all our power came to us from the sacred hoop of the nation, and so long as the hoop was unbroken, the people flourished . . . The sky is round and I have heard that the earth is round like a ball. So are all the stars. The wind, in its greatest power, whirls. Birds make their nests in circles, for theirs is the same religion as ours.

George Armstrong Custer was not thinking of the marvels of circles nor the religion of birds. He was part of a new maneuver to finish the Sioux once and for all. The army had received word from its spies that a large number of Indians were gathering on the plains. A column under General Gibbon was to cross the Yellowstone River and march to the forks of the Big and Little Bighorn rivers. General Custer was to make a wider sweep to prevent the escape of the hostiles. Even before he left on his mission, Gibbon warned Custer not to make any independent or premature attacks.

Custer marched as rapidly as possible in order to be the first to reach the encampment. Without waiting for Gibbon, he divided his 7th Regiment into four groups. Two hundred and twenty-five men were kept under his personal command. Two groups of approximately half that strength were to move parallel to him under the commands of Major Reno and Captain Benteen. Another group of a little over a hundred men was to guard the supply train. Custer's efforts to co-ordinate his columns were scant. Reno was told to attack the camp on sight, an order he followed with a spirited charge in the manner Custer most admired. After a few moments, however, the major realized that he was outnumbered more than ten to one. He moved his men back to higher ground, losing half his command in the heavy fighting. Custer had seen Reno being pushed back, but Custer had his own notion of how best to give relief. Benteen cut short his unsuccessful scouting to reinforce Reno. Some critics suggest Benteen should have gone in search of Custer, but Reno and Benteen expected Custer to relieve *them.*

Custer's fate will never be known for certain, although some facts are clear. Pawnee scouts had informed him that the camp was larger than expected. Custer had been concerned that the Sioux and their allies would flee before he had time to mount an attack. When he sighted a huge cloud of dust in the distance he thought the Indians were already fleeing and he ordered a mounted charge. The attack at full gallop was his favorite, perhaps only, tactic. Custer actually gained entrance to the camp, but this was no group of a hundred or even five hundred lodges. The dust in the distance was a pack train of women and children, while the dust engulfing him was made by a thousand warriors under the leadership of Gall. Either Custer had run straight into an ambush or, most likely, he had met a desperate, spur of the moment countercharge head on. The terrain was difficult and the fighting was mainly on foot. Custer formed his men into a small circle. Contrary to legend, he had no saber and his usually long yellow hair had been clipped short before he left the fort. Within an hour, his entire command perished.

He would later be depicted as the last man to fall, a highly improbable circumstance since every warrior wanted the honor of being his killer. The brave commander would be shown raising his saber, his long hair waving in the wind and arrows sticking from various parts of his body. Custer's widow would strive to propagate this Custer mythology. The Massacre at Sand Creek had not offended the nation's sense of morality even though it was an unprovoked massacre, but Custer's Last Stand, a military defeat brought on by Custer's own offensive action, was considered an outrage. Indians relate that Sitting Bull, still suffering from the pain of his Sun Dance wounds, understood the implications of the afternoon only too well, "Now they will never let us rest."

Reno's position continued to be under heavy attack for several hours but even under leaders such as Crazy Horse and Gall, the Sioux would not fight in complex patterns. Some of the warriors would claim that certain head men wanted Reno spared because if they killed too many bluecoats the army would never forgive them. It is more probable that Reno and Benteen would have shared the fate of Custer and Fetterman if the strong column under Gibbon that Custer was supposed to wait for had not finally appeared to save them.

The Sioux victory was impressive, but soon the Sioux would be scattered like the seeds of a dandelion. Their ammunition was almost all gone. The buffalo herds were greatly reduced, and most other game had been frightened off by the large camp and the burning grass of the military battles. More important than these physical realities, the Sioux had done the unpardonable. The socially and racially inferior "redskins" had annihilated several companies of the best United States cavalry. Such a catastrophe would have been shocking at any time, but it occurred just a few days before the Fourth of July, 1876, the one hundredth jubilee celebration of American Independence. Everywhere whites clamored for quick revenge. A nation's honor was at stake. New armies were sent to destroy the hostiles. These armies were prepared to continue until victory, whether the victory came in the autumn grass or in winter snows at temperatures below zero.

Not many days after the defeat of Custer, Buffalo Bill shot down Chief Yellow Hand to gain new fame as having taken "the first scalp for Custer." He was campaigning under Brevet Major General Merrit, who drove large bodies of Cheyenne back to their Agency in the first weeks of July. Ceaseless rains, mud, and the shortage of rations delayed army retaliation on a grand scale but by August the counterattacks began to hurt. When a camp of Miniconjou was struck, Crazy Horse's band joined in the fighting which took the life of Chief American Horse. In November, Dull Knife's Cheyenne were attacked. Thirty Indians were killed and two hundred lodges destroyed. Meanwhile, General Miles was ready for a winter campaign against Sitting Bull. He outfitted his men with buffalo overcoats and had thick blankets cut into underwear and face masks. In October, a conference was arranged between the two leaders. When no agreement could be reached, Miles ordered an attack. The Hunkpapa put up a spirited running fight for forty-two miles. A part of them agreed they would go to an Agency and surrender, but Sitting Bull remained unbroken. When another of his camps was attacked in December, the oracle decided to lead his followers across the invisible line to Canada.

By the next spring the shortage of game was becoming the major factor in all Indian decision making. They had no pack trains to supply them with food from the east and south. They marched with their entire families wherever they had to go. Crazy Horse saw his supplies dwindling, and his hunters could find no buffalo. He realized he must surrender in order to preserve his people, yet his Oglala came to Fort Robinson with all the pomp of a victorious force. Crazy Horse led a procession of eight hundred warriors in one of the most stirring sights the soldiers had ever witnessed. Each mounted brave appeared in full war paint, wearing his best bonnet, carrying his finest shield, and handling his favorite weapon. The men sang the most powerful songs they knew before ending with their individual death chants, for the death song was a final plea to the Unseen to have pity on an individual and intervene on his behalf. Crook, who was noted for his sensitive handling of Indians, allowed the Oglala this final display of pride before the disarming. He understood how important it was to the warriors that they not be humiliated. He had not been able to defeat them upon the Rosebud. Even now, only the lack of provisions was making them give up. It was enough that the last days of the Vision Seekers were fast being consumed. The general saw no advantage in placing salt in the running wound of their surrender.

Crazy Horse tried to adjust to life at the Agency, but any kind of confinement was a terrible burden on his spirit. Crazy Horse had led the slaughter of Fetterman and he had led the successful foray at the Wagon Box Fight. His rise as a war leader had been rapid as he distinguished himself equally against Indian and white opponents. While he didn't have the rounded wisdom of Sitting Bull, he was not to be manipulated by the whites like Red Cloud. The fighters of 1876 had come to pity that old chief as much as they were angered by his pacifism. They knew that Red Cloud was paraded about in the East to meet dignitaries and to serve as a showpiece, while at home he was constantly cheated and swindled because he could not read or write. Sitting Bull often made remarks about how foolish and trusting Red Cloud was. Crazy Horse was a different sort of personality. He felt the Sioux virtues as a pounding of blood in his temple. He said the whites were so evil they would soon try to pen up the grass.

General Crook had always respected Crazy Horse and he thought that he would honor the chief by allowing him to scout for the army against the Nez Percé, a tribe that had always feuded with the Sioux. Crook reasoned that there was a double advantage in keeping one set of Indians happy by having them serve the United States in a war against other Indians—a move which discouraged intertribal unity. Crazy Horse sent word to Crook that he would fight until all the Nez Percé were killed; but his enemies among the Sioux, who were jealous of his fame, twisted the message to say that Crazy Horse had said he would fight until all the whites were killed. The misunderstanding was eventually cleared up, but many officers never quite trusted Crazy Horse again. Crook thought a personal conference with Crazy Horse would smooth matters, but Crazy Horse's enemies, encouraged by whites in the Indian Bureau and army, again sabotaged the possibility of reconciliation. They told Crook that Crazy Horse planned to kill him when they met, and the general dropped his idea rather than risk new tensions. The involvement of the Nez Percé in the controversy was ironic, for later in the same year, the band led by White Bird would overcome traditional hostilities to unite with Sitting Bull in Canada. Such acts came too late and involved too few Indians to halt their destruction.

Crazy Horse grew more and more despondent. The frustrations of reservation existence were compounded by the death of his young bride. Jealous tribesmen kept him under surveillance and made regular reports about him to the whites. Crazy Horse knew he must bolt from the confining reservation but other warriors persuaded him to attend one more conference. Coming into the actual fort and passing through the gates heightened Crazy Horse's apprehension. Less than a year had passed since the murder of Sioux leaders at Fort Keogh in Montana. When the military told him he must submit to being locked in a guardhouse, Crazy Horse rebelled and reached for his weapons. His own people struggled to subdue him and a soldier stabbed him with a bayonet for "resisting arrest." Crazy Horse died that night after describing the incident to the local agent:

> I was tired of fighting. I went to the Spotted Tail Agency and asked that chief and his agent to let me live there in peace. I came here with the agent to talk with the Big White Chief but was not given a chance. They tried to confine me. I tried to escape and a soldier ran his bayonet into me. I have spoken.

Many years later while living out his own last days in a strange new century, Black Elk would recall the weeping poignancy of the night Crazy Horse was murdered. The slain leader's father took the thirty-year-old body and buried it in some unknown place on the plains. White historians would one day ask where the body was buried. The wise Sioux would reply, "It does not matter where his body lies for it is grass; but where his spirit is, it will be good to be."

When the grasses hid their faces in their mother's bosom in 1877, in all the prairies from Canada to the Gulf there was no longer a free tribe of Sioux. Just forty summers had passed since the boundary of Indian country had been set. The Indians had been promised the white men would never settle beyond the Mississippi. Every solemn pledge had been broken, every treaty torn. For one people, "manifest destiny" meant that their young nation would stretch its iron might from the rising to the setting sun. For other, older nations, it meant all their citizens must sing their death songs. Even Sitting Bull at last grew weary of the cold of the north. He wanted to return to his own land and once more see the faces of friends and relatives. In 1881 he quietly crossed back into the United States and gave up his weapons. As he came in to the confinement, which was deadly to the Sioux soul, he sang,

> A warrior
> I have been.
> Now,
> It is all over.
> A hard time
> I have.

A DREAM DIES

Ten years of reservation life passed in bitterness and pain. The Indians could not adjust to captivity. Then, in 1888, a new wind began to blow from the Nevada deserts. A prophet called Wovoka had dreamed a great dream when he was struck by scarlet fever on the day of a total eclipse of the sun. Different variations of his prophecy spread among the nations, but the basic thread was the same. Wovoka had spoken with the Creator, who had told him that the Indians had not come to the end of the trail. They need only put aside all war and love one another and they would have a special place in the afterlife. The Creator had even given Wovoka a dance to be performed on five successive nights. The more often it was danced, the sooner Judgment Day and the end of the world as it was now known.

As the Ghost Dance moved eastward to where the Sioux lived, its prophecy changed. The suffering earth would die. All races of man would die. But there would be a rebirth. The whites, if reborn at all, would go to some other world. The Indians would return to this world, their own familiar world of grass and buffalo. All the red people who had ever lived would return in the splendor of their youth. Heaven and earth would again be in joyous harmony. One of the chants for the new dance was repeated over and over, "We shall live again. We shall live again."

The new prophecy swept the reservations, and the whites feared the Ghost religion would unite the Indians against them. They did not understand that the Ghost Dance was a religious revival and not a dance for warriors. Men, women, and children danced in order to make a world free of whites, misery, disease, and death. They believed their spiritual power could transform the world. They thought they could dance their enemies into extinction. Old Red Cloud accepted the dance, and soon six thousand Sioux were dancing with him. Their need was so profound that they danced until they fell from exhaustion. They spent hours discussing how soon the end of the world would be.

The agents learned that some of the medicine men were making Ghost shirts which they said no bullet could penetrate. Word spread that the honored Sitting Bull was going to go to Pine Ridge, where he, too, would perform the Ghost Dance. No figure in the Sioux world commanded his personal prestige. People whispered that after Sitting Bull danced, the Sioux would have a victory far greater than

In 1882, a year after his surrender, Sitting Bull was photographed relaxing with his two wives and three children. (*Courtesy of Museum of the American Indian, Heye Foundation*)

the one following his Sun Dance upon the Little Bighorn. The nervous military ordered the Ghost Dance stopped and brought more troops to the reservations.

Sitting Bull was now fifty-six years old. He had traveled with the Buffalo Bill Wild West Show and knew that military victory against the whites was impossible. His decision to explore the full power of the new dance was a spiritual rather than a political act. The Indian Bureau had tried to break his spirit by withholding his rations, but the proud Sitting Bull had never been affected. Many times, to show his contempt for his captors, he didn't bother to report to the agents at all. The military feared this strength. They feared that whatever his personal motives were, any war spirit that lingered in the Sioux would come to life as soon as he danced. Indian police were sent to his house to prevent him from going to Pine Ridge.

The police found Sitting Bull sleeping in his unguarded house. At first he was willing to go with them peacefully, but members of his band gathered and warned him not to go. A few taunted him for being a coward. His seventeen-year-old son told him to resist. The police grew nasty with their words and actions. During those tense moments, Sitting Bull might well have recalled the fate of Dull Knife and Crazy Horse. Suddenly he refused to go with the police and everyone drew his gun. When the shooting stopped, Sitting Bull and his son were among the dead.

News of the killing spread like a prairie fire out of control. Sitting Bull's people fled northward to hide in the Bad Lands of Dakota, fearing they, too, would be murdered in their homes. Some of them encountered a group led by Big Foot, who was just returning to the Agency for supplies. The head man took them in and was terribly upset by their news. A troop under Colonel Forsyth soon overtook them. Big Foot was so ill with pneumonia that he could not ride his horse. His band included no more than one hundred aging and hungry warriors. Only purposeful malice could have misread them as a war party. Big Foot hoisted a white flag for a parley but the army insisted on his unconditional surrender. The band had no choice but to be escorted to a post office near a stream called Wounded Knee Creek.

More troops were sent for until a total of almost five hundred bluecoats with early model machine guns guarded some three hundred sick Indians. The soldiers were stationed above the Indian camp on heights which prevented any chance of escape. Many of them had been with Reno at the Little Bighorn. On December 29, the Indians were gathered in a semicircle and told they must give up their guns. Only two weapons were produced. The soldiers then began searching through the tents in the roughest manner, shoving women over the beds, and acting like bandits.

The massacre area at Wounded Knee, South Dakota, 1890. (*Courtesy of Museum of the American Indian, Heye Foundation*)

They found forty weapons, most of them nearly useless relics from bygone campaigns. A young brave agitated by fear pulled a gun from his blanket and fired at the soldiers. Rational men could have subdued the berserk individual, but the line of blue on the heights only needed just such an excuse to use their machine guns and rifles. Half the Indians must have been killed during the first minutes of fire. The survivors hurled themselves upon the soldiers near them using their knives, clubs, fists, and teeth. The repeating rifles pumped explosive shells into the struggling bodies at a rate of fifty per minute. Within a short time, two hundred Indians and sixty soldiers were dead. Still unsatisfied, the soldiers proceeded to kill any Indian they could find still living. Later, bodies were found more than two miles away. Survivors reported that women and children were enticed from hiding places in the rocks only to be abused and murdered. The final toll of Indian dead ran to over three hundred. Ghost shirts were seized as souvenirs. The troopers bragged loudly that they had avenged Custer.

Resistance by other terrified bands continued for some weeks but eventually General Miles brought peace. The Ghost Dance was finished. Within a few summers more than half the land still owned by the Sioux would be taken. The Indian Bureau would manipulate supplies to starve anyone who would not give up Indian religion and tribal custom. All authority was snatched from the head men and the councils. Children were forced into boarding schools and were often hired out as cheap labor in summer. They were forced to join whatever Christian sect was most influential in their particular school or reservation and they were forbidden to speak any native language or discuss Indian ways. Land was divided into smaller and smaller pieces to destroy all memory of communalism. The Sioux were told how to wear their hair, how to dress, how to behave. The policies of the Indian Bureau were a conscious and systematic attempt to break a nation's soul. Sitting Bull had foreseen it in his surrender speech:

> I do not wish to be shut up in a corral. It is bad for the young men to be fed by an agent. It makes them lazy and drunken. All agency Indians I have seen are worthless. They are neither red warriors nor white farmers. They are neither wolf nor dog. But my followers are weary of cold and hunger. They wish to see their brothers and their old home, therefore I bow my head.

The Sioux suffered more than most tribes because their lives were so fundamentally opposed to the ways of the whites. Reservations were prisons with invisible bars for a people that needed wide territories to wander in. Reservations made the Sioux feel sullen and sluggish. Many turned to drink. Some years later a few would begin to dream again through the use of the peyote drug, but they would never again experience the full glory of the old ways. Black Elk had seen it all: "Sometimes I think it might have been better if we had all stayed together and made them kill us all." But his pessimism was not as strong as his faith in the good spirits and in the order of the universe. Even as he felt the spirit of death drawing near him, Black Elk resolved he must continue to fight. He chose to commit his life to a book, hoping that the vision he had received as a youth might still be realized in some strange and unknown manner. Black Elk, the oracle, had given much thought to the Wounded Knee Massacre. He had been a young man at the time of the incident and had been among those who gathered the dead bodies for burial. The contorted corpses frozen blue and green by ice and snow had so horrified him that he thought he would never be able to dream again. Wounded Knee was the symbol of all the injustice the whites had done to the Indians. Black Elk remembered the day vividly and understood what it meant for all the tribes of North America:

> I did not know then how much was ended. When I look back now from this high hill of my old age, I can still see the butchered women and children lying heaped and scattered all along the crooked gulch as plainly as when I saw them with eyes still young. And I can see that something else died there in the bloody mud, and was buried in the blizzard. A people's dream died there. It was a beautiful dream.
>
> And I, to whom so great a vision was given in my youth—you see now a pitiful old man who has done nothing, for the nation's hoop is broken and scattered. There is no center any longer, and the sacred tree is dead.